YES, YOU CAN TALK ABOUT MENTAL HEALTH AT WORK

TRIGGER™

The mental health & wellbeing publisher

"This book will challenge your thinking. Whether you're a CEO or have just embarked on your first few weeks in the working world – or anything in between, this book is for you. It's intensely practical, with clear and concise pointers to help us all on our journey with talking about mental health at work. Informative and thought-provoking, this book is a must-read."

— *Jonny Combe, UK CEO, PayByPhone*

"With compassion and authority, Melissa addresses the real issues and barriers of why people aren't comfortable sharing about mental health at work, and how to overcome those fears. She highlights so clearly that everyone has mental health, just as we have physical health, and the importance of vocalizing this similarity."

— *Julie Cassidy, Director of Sales East, North America, Bumble and Bumble*

"I've been working in the people space for more than 20 years. When I began my career, talking about mental health in the workplace was just not done. Two decades later, I had hoped we would normalize the discussion. We're not there yet, but with Melissa's book, we might get there. This is a playbook for how to have some of the most difficult discussions imaginable at work. And, it just may help you help to change the world of work."

— *Tracie Sponenberg, Chief People Officer at The Granite Group, Co-Founder of DisruptHR NH, and Co-Founder of HR Rebooted*

"This revolutionary book removes the guesswork and minimizes the uncomfortable nature of having conversations about mental health at work. Melissa leverages her clinical expertise and research-based evidence to provide practical guidance for creating psychologically safe workplaces. After reading this book, I felt informed and empowered. This book will forever change the stigma and negative narratives associated with mental health in the workplace. It should be required reading for Human Resources Management courses."

— *Ricklyn Woods, SHRM-SCP, SPHR, PHRCa, Owner of Ricklyn Woods HR Coaching + Consulting*

"This book is a timely and powerful resource for leaders at all levels that are seeking to truly impact their teams at a deeper level with authenticity, empathy and genuine care for their mental wellbeing. Leading organizations recognize that to truly transform their systems, workforce and, ultimately, profitability, they need to allow for courageous conversations about mental health. Melissa does a great job of outlining actionable steps that are practical for such a complex topic that impacts all of us."

— *César A. Lostaunau, Director of Growth Markets/D&I at CENTURY 21®, and Faculty Member, DEI Coaching Center, The Forum on Workplace Inclusion*

ABOUT THE AUTHOR

Melissa Doman, M.A. is an Organizational Psychologist, former Clinical Mental Health Therapist, and Mental Health at Work Specialist.

Following years of clinical work as a licensed mental health therapist in employee-assistance program, private practice and university settings, Melissa left the clinical sector and turned her focus to consulting and speaking in the worlds of organizational psychology and mental health awareness at work – with one goal in mind: to equip companies, individuals, and leaders to have constructive conversations about mental health in the workplace.

Melissa has spoken, presented, and consulted for international, national, and local organizations and Fortune 500 companies across industries and across the globe – including Salesforce, Legal & General, Charlotte Tilbury, the NHS, and the Independent Publishers Guild. Melissa has been featured as a subject matter expert in national conferences, global summits, international mentoring programs, digital publications, and local television shows. Melissa uses her former clinical experience and current organizational psychology work to inform her practical and solution-focused approach that she uses in her work with companies.

Melissa has impacted thousands of people through her work and is determined to bring the topic of mental health at work to the forefront of everyone's minds in business around the world.

She currently resides in the USA with her husband Matt and their rescue dog Lola. Her hobbies include traveling, salsa dancing, singing, drinking a lot of coffee, and eating lots of cheese.

YES, YOU CAN TALK ABOUT MENTAL HEALTH AT WORK

HERE'S WHY
(AND HOW TO DO IT REALLY WELL)

BY MELISSA DOMAN, M.A.

TRIGGER™
The mental health & wellbeing publisher

This edition published in 2023 by Trigger Publishing
An imprint of Shaw Callaghan Ltd

UK Office
The Stanley Building
7 Pancras Square
Kings Cross
London N1C 4AG

US Office
On Point Executive Center, Inc
3030 N Rocky Point Drive W
Suite 150
Tampa, FL 33607
www.triggerhub.org

Text Copyright © 2021 Melissa Doman
First published by Welbeck Balance in 2021

A CIP catalogue record for this book is available upon request from the British Library
ISBN: 9781837963966
Ebook ISBN: 9781837963973

Typeset by Lapiz Digital Services

To my husband. I couldn't have written this
book without your support.
Thank you for always being by my side.

CONTENTS

Prologue   xiii
Introduction   xix

Part 1: The Why   1
1 Mental Health: What It Is and Why It Matters   3
2 Why Mental Health Matters at Work:
       Challenging Workplace Perceptions   18
3 Where We Have Come From and
       Where We Are Now   31
4 The Roadblocks To Progress Outside of Work   51
5 The Roadblocks To Progress at Work   80
Part 1 Conclusion   98

Part 2: The How   **101**
6 How to Talk About Your Mental Health at Work   103
7 How to Have Conversations About
       Mental Health and Support Colleagues   137
8 Leaders and Managers: How to Set the Tone
       and Discuss Mental Health with Your
       Team Members   167
Part 2 Conclusion   197

Part 3: Workplace Mental Health During Tough Times **199**
9   The Effects of Immense Stress   201
10 COVID-19 and Mental Health   207
11 The Continued Mental Health Impact
        of Racial Inequality   223

A Final Note: What Will Your Impact Be?   245

Acknowledgements   247
Endnotes   249
Useful Resources   257

PROLOGUE

I'm not surprised that I ended up writing this book; I'm only surprised it took me this long. Between the stories I have heard socially, professionally and clinically, and what I experienced personally, I could write an encyclopedic series.

Before I studied counselling psychology and became a clinical mental health therapist, I distinctly remember that mental health "wasn't talked about at work". This wasn't even that long ago – think early 2000s. This sadly faulty logic also applied in many families, schools, and other social systems for a long time.

For years, mental health was seen as a "personal issue" that wasn't meant for the world of work, and if you were "smart", you kept it out of there. I always thought that was odd, given that we literally bring our entire bodies and our brains to work (whether to a physical building or virtually) and we dedicate 35–50 hours a week to the cause.

I remember thinking that it seemed utterly unreasonable and unrealistic to expect people to leave their thoughts and feelings outside of work. Sadly, like many people at the time, I accepted it as the social norm, dictating that I should fall in line with this socially created compartmentalization.

I heard countless stories from co-workers, friends, or even strangers, about how they were sure that if their boss found out how much they had been struggling with their mental health, they'd lose their job. It felt disappointing every time I heard it. As time passed on and society "progressed", even after getting my master's degree in counselling psychology and clinical training, I continued to hear stories of fear from those around me. Nothing had changed, yet.

I too have my own tales of mental health at work and the fear-based logic I applied to myself. I too did not feel safe to talk about, or give myself permission to talk about, my own mental health to most of the managers I had. I shared my feelings with the occasional co-worker here and there, but of course, it was sworn to secrecy because those workplaces didn't really send out a message that it was ok to talk about mental health. Aside from the social norm that conditioned me to keep quiet, I too experienced leadership in the workplace that didn't make me feel psychologically safe to speak up about my own struggles. Some leaders were bullies, emotionally constipated, or were just not equipped to navigate those conversations. Looking back at it now, I think they were doing the best that they could with the skill sets they had and based on where they were in their career journeys.

Those experiences were instrumental learning moments that contributed to my growth, making me personally and professionally passionate about the topic of mental health in the workplace.

After I graduated from my master's program, with hundreds of hours of clinical work already under my belt, I was young, and eager to make an impact. My mind was crammed with infinite diagnostic and treatment modality information that I was eager to use. As I got into clinical practice, I was armed with a desire to help my clients gain insight into what they were experiencing and help them learn how to help themselves.

I received as wide an exposure to different types of diagnoses that the DSM (the clinical criteria guide that mental health professionals use to diagnose clients) as my professors said that I would. Some of my clients were "privately struggling" with some fairly heavy-hitting diagnoses and going about their lives, and jobs, "as usual".

Despite the meaningful counselling work with my clients, it felt like what we were doing was in the shadows. I was the "last stop" on the emotional health train. I was the therapist people saw in private, that they may only have told some close friends or family about – definitely not their wider circle, and of course, not their colleagues or boss.

I remember so many clients telling me about how stressed out they were at work, but how they couldn't tell their employer or boss about how they were feeling, for fear of losing the reputation that they'd spent so long building.

I had to do something to change this ingrained status quo. I wanted to help more people than just an individual or a small group at a time. I wanted to take the discussions I was having with my clients about mental health at work out of the proverbial shadows; to show that they weren't wrong, taboo, or weird. And, to address some of the workplace stressors my clients reported, to see if I could make some sort of preventative educational impact – at the source.

After years of clinical work, I transitioned into traditional organizational psychology, specifically focused on employee, culture, and leadership development and behavior change in the workplace. Through both in-house and consultative roles, I was able to make changes from the inside, from a systemic perspective. I focused on making a wider impact through workplace culture and values development, employee and leadership development training, and professional development coaching.

Quickly, I was able to make some significant changes: creating and updating policy, implementing and facilitating programs, and advising leadership members whose buy-in could affect real change. I was updating perspectives, providing education and working to ensure that workplace conversations, leadership styles, and new workplace norms were infused with more empathy, self-awareness, open-mindedness, and personal accountability.

The changes were highly visible and positive. But, I faced some roadblocks – particularly when it came to the language specifically used around mental health in relation to employee wellbeing. Some managers and senior leadership in companies I provided services for didn't want to name a workshop "Stress Management at Work" or publish an intranet article on mental health because of "that person in accounting" that they were worried would interpret it in the wrong way, but had trouble articulating as to *why*.

I was making progress in and for organizations, and yet, the words mental health, mental illness and stress were still very much taboo, and avoided with impressive tenacity by so many.

Over the years, I started to notice a shift. From 2016 onwards, slowly, but surely – and in different ways around the world – the lightbulb switched on.

In Britain, Prince William and Prince Harry were talking about depression and encouraging British society to move away from the historical "stiff upper lip", because it just wasn't sustainable or healthy anymore. American celebrities and business owners opened up about their clinical anxiety and eating disorders, making a once-private issue very public. Social media was cascading hundreds of stories from individuals about their own journeys with mental health and mental illness.

People were finally starting to talk about mental health, and even their experiences at work! I was ecstatic to be able to actually start talking about the subject – openly – to employers. I could actually talk about mental health at work, and say the actual words "mental health" in the *workplace*.

There was no doubt that people had always wanted to talk about their mental health (I knew that because I was the therapist they talked to). But, finally, the social permission had been given. Now I could blend my organizational experience with my clinical experiences and education, to take the topic of mental health beyond just private conversations, and into the workplace.

I had one goal in mind: to help companies, leaders and individuals understand that discussing mental health at work is a non-negotiable and must-have discussion; normalizing and destigmatizing conversations about mental health, mental illness and stress at work. I began delivering countless keynotes, workshops and training modules, consulting on projects, writing articles and doing media interviews.

Those years of educating, speaking, and consulting have led me here: to this book, in which I hope to create a deep-dive all-in-one reference for those who want to understand the context of the difficulties around discussing mental health at work – and learn *how* to actually have the conversation.

Before we start, I want to remind you of an important phrase that has taken the world by storm in recent years: it's ok not to be ok.

Even more importantly, it's ok to not be ok *at work*, and we need to remind each other of this *at work*.

You don't need to be a mental health therapist to make an impact here. You just need to be an empathetic human, seeking to understand, and willing to help. I'm confident that you are.

INTRODUCTION

WHO IS THIS BOOK FOR?

This book is for any employee, manager, or leader – no matter the industry – who wants to understand mental health at a deeper level and learn how to talk about mental health at work in a constructive and empathetic way.

Individuals: You don't need to be in a leadership position or have a team reporting to you to make an impact. Making a colleague feel safe enough to feel heard can come from anyone. The example that you can set, potentially inspiring others to follow suit, can make positive waves no matter where you sit within an organization. Your impact matters, no matter what role you hold.

Managers: As you sit in a position of influence and visibility, you have opportunities to create an impact on a systemic level. You may have teams or even entire divisions that look to you for leadership. You have access to countless moments where you can let people know that not only can they speak about mental health to you, but also to each other, and that these conversations are not only ok, but *encouraged*.

Management teams and company founders: This book will highlight your ability to set the tone from the top down in your organization, starting with *your* beliefs, actions, and conversations. It will show you how you can reshape the narrative of mental health at work and have a positive influence throughout your organization.

THE CHALLENGES OF DIFFERENT INDUSTRIES

I believe every single industry should have discussions about mental health. But as with any big social change, it comes in fits and starts, and is stronger in some areas than others.

In some industries, the acceptability of discussing mental health has gained traction faster than in others. I've seen this to be particularly visible in creative industries, higher education, customer services, and the automotive and retail industries, to name a few.

There has even been headway made in technology, finance, and law – although this comes with some hesitation as the institutional pressure to perform high-stakes tasks quickly has historically come with an unsaid, or sometimes explicitly said, expectation of not "cracking" under pressure.

There are plenty of industries where it's sadly still widely believed that having a diagnosed mental health condition, being chronically stressed, or expressing any distressing emotions is seen as a sign of weakness or an inability to do the job. I've witnessed this sentiment particularly within medicine, government, politics and law. These industries, in my experience, seem to exude a stance that, with people's lives in your hands, there is *no room* for human imperfection or emotional variance. I remember a virtual session I led at the start of the pandemic, on the importance of normalizing mental health discussions in healthcare for a group of doctors and nurses of the NHS. It was clear they wanted to have the discussion – they just needed the permission to say that they didn't feel ok.

I would *never* aim to generalize entire industries (there are plenty of companies or organizations within industries that go against what I've highlighted), and that's why individual impact and leadership in those individual companies is so important: to help break the stronghold that has kept people silent.

Despite the challenges, people in every industry *have the right* to discuss mental health at work. Your industry may be very progressive and forward thinking; or it may be traditional and immovable. There will be a different set of challenges for each person who reads this book, and I'm very conscious of that. Some readers will have more work to do than others. But industry specificities aside, change is needed across the board.

WHAT ARE WE AIMING TO ACHIEVE?

A very important point here: the aim is not for every single person to be obligated to discuss mental health or mental illness at work. That mandated approach would be counterproductive and make a lot of people feel uncomfortable in a very unhelpful way. What we are aiming for is for every person to feel that they have the *option, permission,* and that they *feel safe* to discuss it.

By reconstructing how we look at mental health and mental illness overall, we can change the conversations we have at work. We can improve how people feel at work and how we connect with one another. Ultimately, we can build a culture that says that it's ok to talk about the shades of grey and complexities of life, and support colleagues so they can do their best work.

This book may not be able to eradicate the silence surrounding mental health at work entirely (no individual or book could do that). But what it *can* do is empower *you*, as an individual, regardless of your position within a company, to further the discussion about mental health and contribute to a positive, non-judgmental environment in your workplace.

This isn't a book about boosting employee engagement or productivity. It's not a book about how employee wellbeing is tied to profits. The link between mental health and those concepts is already widely proven and not my focus here.

Instead, I want to teach you how to shift the workplace cultural fabric around mental health at work through compassionate and constructive conversations. This book will show you the deeper *why*, and the *how*.

This stuff isn't done quickly. Changing a culture and entrenched social norms is effortful and requires patience, strength, and vulnerability. At the risk of sounding trite, this is a marathon not a sprint. Just as you learned to walk, you'll need to take this one step at a time. And most importantly, it's crucial that we get it *right*.

THE GOLD-STANDARD OF MENTAL HEALTH AT WORK

Here's what I believe truly embracing mental health at work looks like, and what the book aims to help you work toward.

Leaders:

- Are emotionally intelligent, vulnerable, and open about their own struggles to their staff, and to other leaders.
- Feel encouraged by the company to prioritize their mental health so they can feel emotionally healthy and be a great leader for their teams.
- Understand that being a leader doesn't mean that they are expected to be faultless and steadfast 100% of the time.

The Entire Staff:

- Can come to work as their whole self – and not feel the need to hide certain parts of who they are.
- Are empowered to speak up about mental health issues, to take mental health days as needed, and use company resources – just as you would for physical health. This narrative is crystal clear throughout the company.
- Show basic care and empathy to one another.

"The support I get from the team around me is unprecedented. From day one, there was such an openness around mental health. It was clear that if you needed help, you could speak up, and that message was backed up by tangible actions. The fact that I can say to my team, 'I'm not doing ok today' is gold. We all speak the same language. The enormous psychological safety these experiences have brought about has been transformative for me personally and professionally."
L, book interviewee (more on these interviews shortly)

MY APPROACH

In this book I will draw on my years of clinical experience as a therapist and my organizational psychology work for companies. I'm going to reference researched-backed information and qualitative lived experiences from people about mental health at work, and the human condition.

I'm conscious that there are a variety of ways to approach this topic, but here's how I see it: before we look into *how* we make changes, we must fully unpack the *why*, with a realistic view of our current environment, and where we've evolved from. Once we have established this, we will go on to look at *how* we can have really worthwhile, authentic conversations about mental health at work, and how you can change your own, and other people's, perceptions around mental health and mental illness, one moment at a time. And, we'll have a look at some additional considerations around mental health at work during *really* tough times.

I aim to demystify this incredibly complex topic, so it feels accessible and actionable. Some of this information may be familiar to you; other elements you may never have considered before. I want to equip you with concrete actions you can use today – your impact can start right now.

THE IMPORTANCE OF LIVED EXPERIENCE

Within the subject of mental health, it's important to hear from real people, with real stories. To this end, I've included a series of interviews throughout the book, so you can learn from the perspectives of many. We'll hear from those who have or have had a mental health condition or chronic stress and felt afraid to talk about it at work at different points in their career, whether self-imposed or due to their company culture. We'll hear about how their culture, gender, religious upbringing, and family dynamics was, and still sometimes is, the voice in their head saying whether or not they have permission to speak up. We'll learn about what these people wish their peers or manager knew about mental health and the simplest gestures someone could make that could make all the difference. And here's a real kicker: of the many interviews I conducted for this book, only *one person* had a positive mental health at work story. One.

These testimonies help show us the conversations that those with mental health conditions, chronic stress, and even just intense transient reactions to life's challenges, are craving to have at work, from both a leader and employee perspective. I hope what they share gives you some insight into the moments they felt, the weight they carried and the reactions from others that they experienced.

I have included the experiences of people from all walks of life, some of whom you would never guess have a diagnosed mental illness or searingly high stress levels from the outside looking in. These stories are de-identified and anonymous. With the approval from the interviewees, I've included the ethnicity and gender that they identify as, and industry, to show that mental health issues impact everyone, no matter who you are or where you come from.

As with all stories, these are very personal to the people who shared them. They do not represent the entirety of their gender, culture, ethnicity, religion or industry. However, including these identifiers is important, to show that mental health experiences are a human issue, regardless of background.

YOUR ROLE

We all come to the topic of mental health with our own ideas and exposure levels. You will have your own experience of mental health or mental illness, and your own motivation for why you want to learn more about the topic. Perhaps your interest in the subject has been sparked by your own experience of clinical depression or intense, long-standing stress at work. Maybe you've seen a colleague struggle with addiction. You may have friends who have mental health conditions who keep it quiet, and it's made you realize there are many people just like them. Or maybe you are aware of the shifting times we're living in and want to learn how best to help in your workplace.

No matter where you're at, or why you're here, thank you for wanting to deepen your learning so you can make an impact. Please be patient and kind to yourself on this learning journey. Just as you would develop any other skill, it takes time, dedication, and practice. However, don't be afraid to take action after you've read this book. Learning without action will not bring about change.

If you haven't experienced a mental health condition yourself, you are still very much able to encourage someone to feel safe to talk about their mental health and offer support – just as you would for any other health condition someone is experiencing. Regardless of your personal experience, what's most important is that you approach the conversation with compassion, empathy, and non-judgment.

I encourage you to critically think about the concepts and advice covered in this book: to assess how you can take them into your unique workplace situation and find what works for you; to take the conversation scripts and use them in a way that *sounds like you*. There are resources listed throughout and in the Useful Resources section at the back of the book. I encourage you to research, read, and research some more, so that this book is a stepping stone in your long-term learning journey.

ACTIONING YOUR LEARNING

I have included practical tasks throughout the book to encourage you to reflect on and action your learning. These exercises can help highlight what is most important to you, and, crucially, what you want to do with this information. The tasks are best utilized if you do them in order, as they're designed to build your awareness and change your perception in Part 1, so you can then act in a constructive way in Part 2.

The tasks in Part 1 are reflection based and often involve having information-seeking conversations outside of work (a chance to practice conversations before applying them in the workplace). Try to complete the tasks when you have some time and space with no major distractions. You might want to go for a walk or find a quiet area of your home – you know where you reflect best.

The tasks in Part 2 are action oriented and designed to be conducted inside the workplace. When starting to action your learning, sometimes the hardest part is taking the first step, like a bird out of the nest for the first time. Have faith in yourself that once you step off the ledge, you will fly, even if it takes you a moment to let your wings expand.

The tasks in Part 3 are *both* learning and action oriented, as this section covers complex mental health topics impacting the workplace that have significantly impacted people. The good news is, you'll have the knowledge and tools from Parts 1 and 2 to equip you for these tasks.

Be mindful of your learning style and what helps you to be most successful when developing a new mindset and skill set. For those of you who are opinion-gatherers and cerebral discussers (like me), you may want to discuss the exercises with a close friend or family member to get their take on them. Ultimately, you will decide how you digest these topics and exercises, but sometimes it's good to look through the prism from a different angle and through the eyes of others.

As with learning any new skill, or broadening your perspective, please be patient and kind to yourself. Change is not linear and there will be natural ups and downs in your growth process as you move through this book. The last thing I want you to feel is bad about your first attempt at this not going as you hoped. All of the experiences and conversations you will have from reading this book provide invaluable learning and growth opportunities. Each moment can make an impact.

This is a Rubik's Cube topic that has evolved, and will continue to do so, over a very long period of time. With that being said, please remember this: how you contribute to this movement counts. Each conversation adds to a collection of conversations that help to change the direction of this evolving narrative.

As the old Tanzanian proverb says, "Little by little, a little becomes a lot."

PART 1

THE WHY

1

MENTAL HEALTH

What It Is and Why It Matters

Before we can start changing the culture of a workplace around the topic of mental health, we need to understand its larger context and debunk some popular social assumptions. So, let's start by defining the term "mental health" and look at some of the terminology we use around the subject.

To live means being exposed to a spectrum of experiences. Some moments are light and easy, and others are as dark as a black hole that could crush you. All of these moments are a part of life and come along with being human. Life works in shades of grey, so it's crucial to look at mental health across this spectrum of experience.

The concepts of mental health, mental illness, and stress have been used interchangeably, in error, over the years – thus creating the confusion that many people have felt surrounding this terminology. That has thankfully started to change, and in recent years, society has sought more clarity about these terms.

What's interesting is that these concepts have grown and evolved throughout human history, from what they mean, to what they *imply*, and misconceptions have even led to some people questioning if they're "real". With such confusion over the basic concept of mental health, it's no wonder some question what's "normal", and what is "ok" to talk about without fear of judgment.

In Chapters 2 and 3, we'll look at the historical picture that's been painted around mental health that led us to the social narrative that we now know (and are consciously trying to change). First, let's look at the present-day definitions.

WHAT IS MENTAL HEALTH?

There are different definitions throughout the world of what the term "mental health" means, and it can mean different things to different people. To keep it simple, let's stick to a mainstream definition that's widely known and used. Mentalhealth.gov, the centralized mental health education information site for the US Department of Health and Human Services, defines mental health as:

> "Our emotional, psychological, and social well-being. It affects how we think, feel, and act. It also helps determine how we handle stress, relate to others, and make choices. Mental health is important at every stage of life, from childhood and adolescence through adulthood."[1]

By this definition, we *all* have mental health.

Just as you have heart health, sexual health, bone health, and the dozens of other kinds of health you have in your body, you have mental health. Your brain, and its functioning, is very clearly on this list.

To be alive, interact with our environment, and possess emotions, is to have mental health. It's the emotional reactions, thoughts, and social interactions related to experiencing life, loss, happiness, neutrality, and everything in between.

And, just like any other organ in the body, our brains can be pushed beyond some limits and develop illness too. Unlike our physical health, mental health is something we can't see, and this may be where the issue lies.

"Mental health is the same as physical health in that we all have natural wear and tear. If you think about what we go through in a lifetime, there is no doubt it will impact our mental health. Our resilience levels can be up or down; mental health challenges will happen to all of us at certain points in our lives. Mental health may mean different things to different people, but at the end of the day, we all have it."
L, a Black female working in the consulting industry

THE NORMAL SPECTRUM OF EMOTIONS

We've established that we all have mental health. Now, we also need to accept that our mental health will naturally include a spectrum of emotion: both positive and negative. To experience negative emotions is well within the expected range of human behavior. Feelings of sadness, anger, worry – and more – are part of the natural variants of emotions within the mental health spectrum.

Not only are negative emotions natural, but they serve an evolutionary purpose, as a form of promoting survival. Negative emotions provide signposts that you may need to disengage from a person, activity, or situation and show to others that you may need support or are in distress. Typically, when someone cries or gets angry, it behaviorally signals to others that that person is in need of attention. And, from a personal perspective, these emotions also signpost to you that your mind needs some care.

In 1982, psychologist Dr. Gloria Willcox created *The Feeling Wheel*[2] to show the basic breakdown of the natural six emotional categories we have: sad, mad, scared, peaceful, powerful, and joyful. Notice that half of these natural base emotions are inherently seen as *negative*. Dr. Wilcox then drilled into each category to show that there are literally dozens of sub-emotions we feel in those categories, naturally.

For sadness alone there are 12 sub-emotions, including feeling inadequate, miserable, and inferior. And yet, many people feel worried about experiencing these emotions, thinking there is something wrong with them. They assume that these deep, complex feelings are beyond the healthy scope of the mental health spectrum.

Well, they're not. And it's this misconception that stops the discussion of these normal negative emotions in everyday life.

However, if those negative feelings and emotions start to become regularly occurring, intensify, and start to impact overall functioning, that is when someone may be edging toward a mental health condition, also known as a mental health disorder or mental illness.

WHAT IS MENTAL ILLNESS?

Mental illness, its cause, and how to treat it is one of the most heavily debated issues in psychiatry, general healthcare, alternative medicine, and psychology today. To simplify this nuanced subject, I am going to use the most up-to-date definition from a reputable source, The Mayo Clinic:

> "Mental illness, also called mental health disorders, refers to a wide range of mental health conditions — disorders that affect your mood, thinking and behavior. Many people have mental health concerns from time to time. But a mental health concern becomes a mental illness when ongoing signs and symptoms cause frequent stress and affect your ability to function."[3]

According to the World Health Organization (WHO), one in four people worldwide will be impacted by a diagnosed mental health condition at some point in their lives.[4] That's not a small portion of the population: that's roughly 1.9 billion people worldwide based on the current population. Clearly this isn't an issue of a small portion of humanity. It's prevalent, it's here to stay, and it's everywhere – even if people aren't talking about it.

There are many people, myself included, who would also venture to say that these numbers may be underreported and are based on those who self-identify and seek treatment. Sadly, not everyone who experiences mental health issues seeks treatment. Not everyone recognizes they have a problem, knows how (or wants) to put into words what they're experiencing or has access to resources.

HAVING A MENTAL ILLNESS IS NOT A CHOICE

There is a very long list of potential causes that can kick off the development of a mental illness, all of which are beyond someone's control (see page 9). Having a mental illness is not a choice. Just as you wouldn't choose to develop Type 1 diabetes or Crohn's disease, you wouldn't choose to develop neural pathways in the brain that lead to a mental illness.

And the ability to cope with a mental illness is also subject to a number of factors, some of which are out of our control. These could include education about what mental illness is, recognition of having a problem, or access to counselling or medication. There are many people who experience mental illness, and due to being socially marginalized or located in an area where resources aren't available, cannot get access to the care they need.

People can be quick to question why those with mental illnesses don't just "sort themselves out", seek support and get better, when the picture is often far more complicated than that.

"If I could not be sad, I would not be sad. It's not like I'm trying to be depressed." K, a mixed-background female (Black and Caucasian) working in administrative support

It's important to note that someone *experiences* a mental illness, not that they're *suffering* from a mental illness. You, hopefully, wouldn't say that someone is suffering from diabetes, but rather, that they *have* diabetes. To say that someone is suffering from mental illness stigmatizes it further and makes it seem as though it's the *entirety* of who they are, which is not the case.

"Treat it like any other illness. It is another illness… Don't treat it as if it's some kind of threat." R, a Caucasian male lawyer

WHO CAN EXPERIENCE A MENTAL ILLNESS?

No matter who you are or where you come from, mental illness knows no boundaries. It affects people from all walks of life.

There are some common misconceptions and stereotypes where people assume that mental illness tends to reside in the "extremes" in society (e.g. the "mad" genius or the schizophrenic homeless person). While mental illness absolutely exists in those groups, it is just as prevalent in the general population, amongst the people that we know and interact with every day. It may just be that these people experience mental illness silently, and you wouldn't know they have it unless they shared it with you.

I challenge you to take any pre-existing notions you may have around the "type" of person who would have mental illness and toss it out the door. There is no "type" of person that experiences mental illness. It can affect anyone, from anywhere, anytime.

WHY DO SOME PEOPLE EXPERIENCE MENTAL ILLNESS?

There are many reasons why a mental illness may develop. There is no singular cause because it's not a linear problem. No two people are identical in this and the influencing factors that usher a person down the pathway of developing a mental illness, while sometimes similar, are unique.

To give you a general sense, mental illness develops from a variety of coalescing factors and how they interplay with each other. In other words, it doesn't come from just one thing.

Mental illness usually develops from a genetic predisposition, trauma, abuse, neglect, or prolonged stress. The environment in which we grow up, or the people we encounter in our formative years, can also influence how a mental illness can develop.

To show you how truly complex this can really be, have a look at the below list of the different factors that can impact someone developing a mental illness. Organizations like Mind UK[5] and the Centers for Disease Control (CDC)[6] highlight the following as different ways that mental illness can develop:

- Early adverse life experiences, such as trauma or a history of abuse (e.g. child abuse, sexual assault, neglect, witnessing violence, etc.)
- Experiences related to other ongoing chronic physical medical conditions (e.g. cancer or diabetes)
- Chemical imbalances in the brain
- Genetic predisposition (e.g. Bipolar Disorder, Schizophrenia, and addiction)

- Prolonged use of alcohol or recreational drugs
- Social isolation and feelings of loneliness
- Sexual or physical abuse
- Experiencing discrimination and stigma
- Social disadvantage, poverty, or debt
- Bereavement
- Unemployment or losing a job
- Homelessness
- Having long-term caregiving responsibilities (e.g. caring for an ill relative in isolation for years on end)
- Domestic violence
- Being bullied
- Significant trauma as an adult (e.g. being in combat, an accident, or the victim of a crime)
- A head injury

When I think about the above factors and how mental illness can develop, I've always conceptualized it by looking at the brain, and our nervous system, as one big tape recorder. (Yes, I realize I'm dating myself here as an '80s baby.) We're constantly on "record". If we press the different buttons too many times, throw the machine around, or use it haphazardly, it can wear on the machine and the tape material. It can still "work" and function, but not as easily it's supposed to. That's how I look at mental health conditions. Someone can still function, but not as smoothly or easily as they'd like to.

SPECIFIC DIAGNOSES

It might surprise you to know that there are nearly 300 different defined mental disorders in the DSM-5, the *Diagnostic and Statistical Manual of Mental Disorders – 5th Edition*.[7] That's a lot! Some of the clinical diagnoses that are most well known and socially discussed are around depression, anxiety, addiction, eating disorders, substance abuse, personality disorders, trauma, schizophrenia, bipolar and psychosis.

There is a school of thought that mental illness is over-medicalized. I understand this and agree that slapping a diagnosis on everything is not the answer, especially not on short-term, reasonable, healthy negative emotions in response to a stressful event. This just serves to undermine the helpful truth that negative emotions are part of the mental health spectrum (see page 5). However, it is important to remember that for some people who have been searching for a long time, trying to understand what it is they are feeling, it can be comforting to be able to name what it is that's happening – because then they can finally gain insight and learn how to manage it.

A mental health diagnosis is both an art and a science. The science piece is the medical nomenclature and thought processes to understand the constellation of symptoms that have shown up, to understand how someone's emotions, behaviors, thoughts, and cognitions have formed unhealthy coping patterns and adaptations.

The art is then *how* that diagnosis is used, in conjunction with counselling and sometimes medication, as a tool to help someone understand what they are experiencing and take next steps on how to manage it. A diagnosis is just part of who someone is and can impact how they see the world, but it is not the entirety of who they are.

"Major depression is very real and it's something that washes over you when it's occurring. It doesn't define me as a person. It's part of who I am, it's part of who many people are. It's something I know how to deal with. I may need accommodation from time to time, but ultimately I can self-service this part of who I am." F, a Caucasian male working in the software industry

HOW MIGHT SOMEONE EXPERIENCE A MENTAL ILLNESS?

It's important to note that while a diagnosis has a typical set of characteristics, how it manifests can be unique to the individual. So, if someone were to tell you that they have Major Depressive Disorder, I would encourage you to seek to understand what that looks like specifically for *that person* instead of assuming that they are experiencing a certain set of symptoms.

Mental illness can manifest in different phases of life, whether it's childhood, adolescence, young adulthood, or adulthood. It all depends on the factors, circumstances, and how they combine. You could have it for a lifetime, or for just a few months, or on and off again. There's not one specific mold. Mental illness shows up differently for different people, ranging from mild to debilitatingly severe, and everything in between.

D, an Indian male who works in the software development industry, shares about the effects of his Generalized Anxiety Disorder:

> "I'm uneasy all the time. It affects your sleep, confidence at work, social life, sometimes I'm even fearful to go out. At its worst, when I'm having a panic attack, I sweat, and get pins and needles. I can't concentrate or focus on anything. I turn very quiet. It's difficult to get my words out. On bad days, it happens multiple times a day. On good days, I just get on with my normal regular life." D

R is a Caucasian male lawyer with diagnosed Major Depressive Disorder:

> "There's rarely a day where I'm not aware of it in some form. There have been very few days since I was 12 years old where I wasn't thinking, 'I wish I wasn't here.' It's

become so much the norm that the thoughts are not as dramatic to me as they appear to be. That's just the way it is. It's as though you're pulling this great big weight behind you." R

K is a mixed-background female (Black and Caucasian) who works in administrative support. She has Post-Traumatic Stress Disorder (PTSD), Generalized Anxiety Disorder and Major Depressive Disorder:

"With my depression and anxiety, when I wake up, I wonder which one will be in the forefront. Most of the time it's depression. With the depression comes an inability to prioritize or be motivated to do my work. For me, the hardest thing I have is that I can be all ready to work, but then the act of just getting up leads me to think, 'Why bother?' With that, it's incredibly difficult to complete a task. On bad days, I don't get out of bed, I don't talk to anybody." K

Another important piece to note is that when someone is experiencing more intense symptoms from their mental health condition, or an episode, sometimes their "good/ neutral" thought processes may be suspended and they're unable to re-center themselves, if you will. So, saying things like "cheer up" to a depressed person or "calm down" to an anxious person is not only unhelpful, but denies the emotional, physiological and neurological experience that person is going through. And, don't you think they would do those things if they could?

HIGH OR LOW FUNCTIONING

Some forms of mental illness are very intense, unpredictable, dangerous, and heavily impact a person's functioning to the point where they can't manage their condition, complete daily tasks, or integrate with society. This is referred to as low functioning mental illness. This may include:

- Someone who is on long-term disability for mental health issues and cannot work
- Someone who has to be in a long-term inpatient behavioral health unit in a hospital that has staff who will provide them with therapy multiple times a week, medication, and supervise their daily activities for safety reasons
- Someone whose mental health condition is so bad that they cannot maintain a job, relationships, or a home and – very sadly – end up on the street

Typically speaking, you're less likely to see low functioning mental illness in the workplace, although it does occur.

The majority of people who struggle with mental illness are high functioning. This means they can engage in and maintain employment, financial responsibility, travel, meaningful relationships and romantic partnerships, raising a family (if they choose to have children), and all of the other #adulting marker things we all do.

TREATING MENTAL ILLNESS

There are myriad of medical treatments, medications, talking therapies and experiential therapies available to treat and manage mental illness that are constantly evolving. Some research institutions in different countries are even experimenting with micro-dosing of once-illegal substances (e.g. THC, psilocybin and MDMA) for the treatment of mood disorders and trauma, some studies of which have shown a massive reduction in patients' symptoms.

But when it comes to mental illness, it's often not about finding a "cure". It's about aiming for a better understanding of the condition, promoting insight, and encouraging awareness and management of symptoms. Of course it would be great if there was a quick and easy fix for mental health conditions, but this is not the plane of existence we live in. We need to play the game with the cards we've been dealt in this human life.

Additionally, some people may be unwilling to acknowledge or manage their mental illness. An unpopular thing to say, but as someone who witnessed this time and time again in my work, it is a fact of life.

MENTAL ILLNESS AND STRESS ARE NOT THE SAME THING

Before we move on, there's one more important differentiator we need to cover: that stress and mental illness, contrary to popular belief, are different.

I mentioned earlier that people often use the terms stress and mental illness interchangeably – and that's when we arrive at incorrect assumptions. Some people believe that stress is mental illness. Let's debunk that myth right now. Stress, or chronic stress, is not mental illness.[8] It may present in similar ways (e.g. emotional distress, negative emotions happening more often, etc.), but it is not the same. These responses are our body and mind communicating to us that we need to release the proverbial pressure valve and engage in some self-care – but, it is not a diagnosable mental illness, and not listed in the DSM-5. If left unmanaged, chronic stress could *turn into* mental illness (e.g. an Adjustment Disorder). But, stress or chronic stress, is not mental illness.

Stress is normal, it's part of life, and we all encounter it in some way, shape, or form – almost every day of our life. Moreover, stress is something that we encounter when we are met with a stimulus that requires change or adjustment. That's what it is to live: we encounter different stimuli all the time and adjust as required. Sometimes it's an easy adjustment, and other times it's gut wrenching, and everything in between. But the point here is this: stress is normal and unavoidable. As such, discussions about stress and its impact on mental health and mental illness need to be part of the mental health at work conversation.

Now that we've addressed the concepts around mental health, in the next chapter we'll take a look at why mental health matters at work, and – importantly – why we need to change workplace perceptions around mental health and mental illness.

TASK
Reflect Upon Your Opinions of Mental Health and Mental Illness

Before you can run, you need to walk. In this case, you must reflect and be aware of how the information in this chapter has confirmed or changed your opinions, biases, or thoughts on mental health and mental illness, before you can act on trying to support someone in a constructive way.

Consider the following questions, and note down your answers.

- Has this chapter changed how you think about mental health? If so, why? How did you view the concept of mental health before and after reading this chapter?
- Has this chapter changed how you think about mental illness? If so, why? How did you view the concept of mental health before and after reading this chapter?

- Do you know anyone with a diagnosed mental health condition? Have you made assumptions about them or their behaviors? If so, what were these assumptions and why did you think that way?
- What new beliefs do you want to take forward about mental health and mental illness?

While this task is reflection based, it sets up the foundation for the practical steps and actions you'll take later in this book.

CHAPTER SUMMARY

- We all have mental health. It's our baseline social, emotional and cognitive functioning.
- Our baseline spectrum of emotions includes negative emotions too.
- Mental illness is a disorder that affects your mood, thinking and behavior. One in four people will experience this in their lifetime. Mental illness can be low or high functioning.
- There are over 300 mental health diagnoses – but diagnosis isn't about finding a cure – it's about promoting insight and self-management of symptoms.
- Having a mental illness is NOT a choice.
- Anyone can develop mental illness, from a variety of causes, and it looks different for everyone.
- It's important to separate the illness from the person.
- Stress is normal and not a mental illness.

2

WHY MENTAL HEALTH MATTERS AT WORK

Challenging Workplace Perceptions

We've established that everyone experiences mental health, that anyone can experience a mental illness, and that their experience of it will be unique and complex. We have also established the prevalence of mental illness – it's extremely common. And as we bring all of ourselves to work – mind, body, experiences and more – we bring our mental health and mental illness into work, too.

So, it follows that mental health can affect your work. And that having a mental illness could possibly make certain jobs harder. But get this: it's even possible that having certain types of mental illness can be helpful at work. This is something worth noting since most people don't associate mental illness with a potentially positive outcome.

Ultimately, the exact effect of someone's mental health or mental illness on their work will depend on many factors, including: the type of condition they have, the type of role, their relationship with their manager and team, the demand of responsibilities, and the environment of the company.

In this chapter, we'll look at why mental health matters at work, and explore and update some of the perceptions around the subject, including:

- The need to acknowledge that mental health and mental illness IS a workplace issue.
- How we view mental health and mental illness within the context of work.
- What mental health struggles can look like at work.

IS MENTAL HEALTH A WORKPLACE ISSUE?

No surprise here, my answer is unequivocally: yes, it absolutely is. We need to remove this unreasonable work/life partition.

To play devil's advocate, from a purely transactional perspective, I understand (but very much *disagree*) with the view of many business owners that mental health or mental illness is *not* a workplace issue. Speaking in sweeping generalizations, consider this. At a company, you're hired to fill a specific role, to produce specific results, and to add value to the company, thus fulfilling their business plan and purpose. Here's a visual representation:

$$A \text{ (person)} + B \text{ (role)} = C \text{ (results)}$$

However, the problem with this simple equation is that it doesn't take into account the multitude of human factors that play into part A and how A does part B. In fact, it's more like:

$$A \text{ (person)} + A1 \text{ factor} + A2 \text{ factor} + A3 \text{ factor} + A4 \text{ factor} + A5 \text{ factor} + B \text{ (role)} = C \text{ (results)}$$

It's something that businesses have had to learn over time, to understand how the *whole person* impacts that equation; most importantly, how the workforce, over time through opening up, has expressed a desire to discuss those factors and feel released from the pressure to keep their life separate for the sake of "professionalism". That work/life partition, also known as "compartmentalization", is, for many people, slowly becoming a practice of the past.

> *"You have to understand your employees and what you're asking of them. I can produce quality work and keep going, but it isn't sustainable. You have to be understanding toward people's lives and the way they individually function."* E, a Caucasian female working in the tourism industry

L also had some interesting comments about this limiting transactional approach when she worked for a startup that pushed its employees to the brink, because there was a "job" to get done, no matter what:

> *"It's not that the founders weren't good people – it's not that simple. Employee wellbeing just wasn't on their agenda. Their focus was: how can we go faster, hit the milestones we've set, and how can we get the best out of people by pushing them harder?"* L, a Black female working in the consulting industry

In Chapter 3, I set out my three reasons Why We Need To Get It Right (page 47). These reasons enforce the argument that mental health *is* a workplace issue. From a human, caring perspective – and also from a business perspective.

ERODING COMPARTMENTALIZATION
Compartmentalization, the idea that work is wholly separate from *everything else* (e.g. life), once firmly in place, functioned as a way of keeping anything personal out of work because it

was the "professional" thing to do. For this to work in practice, work expectations and outcomes must be linear. And life is definitely *anything but* that.

Just as companies realized over time that people at work are far from linear, many people came to realize that this concrete divide was unrealistic, unhealthy and out of date. To spend 35+ hours a week with people and have to compartmentalize mental health (and definitely mental illness) out of that world was, and is, unsustainable. This is not to say that *some* compartmentalization isn't reasonable. It definitely can be, and it has its place, especially for those who prefer to be more private. However, when compartmentalization is so rigid and limiting, it can become a roadblock to constructive mental health conversations.

Think about the consistent energy it took (and still takes) for people to keep that separation. Not only did people keep their "whole self" out of work, but it also meant not fully showing up at work.

TASK
Do You Compartmentalize?

Pause for a moment and ask yourself:
- Do you compartmentalize between work and "life"?
- If yes, why do you do that?
- Does compartmentalizing serve you well?
- Do you compartmentalize about your general mental health or your mental health condition?
- Could compartmentalizing *less* make your colleagues feel like they could take their walls down too?

From your answers, consider any action you can take. Do you want to change how much you compartmentalize your mental health? If so, what do you specifically want to open up about and why?

The culture around compartmentalization has thankfully evolved, and workplaces have become more "humanized" over time. We use our minds at work, and with that comes our experiences, triggers, emotions – our lives. But if you want to compartmentalize – and many do – consider what areas of your life you want to keep separate and be clear on that reason. It shouldn't be because you feel you need to hide your mental health at work.

MENTAL ILLNESS DOES NOT MAKE SOMEONE WEAK OR UNPRODUCTIVE

Having a mental illness doesn't make someone weak or entirely different from other people. These unhelpful and harmful stereotypes about mental illness serve to undermine progress made to further mental health conversations at work.

These incorrect assumptions include, but are not limited to, that someone having a mental illness is:

- Lazy
- Weak
- Can't cope with life
- Can't be productive at work (this is a *big* one, more on this below)
- Can't be a useful contributor to society
- Is potentially dangerous

You can probably think of other (ridiculous) subjective conclusions that you've heard people make about someone with a mental illness. You may have even held these views yourself. It's ok, we all make mistakes.

"You're not less of an employee or less capable. You are not less productive or employable. You're not going to be

a hindrance to the team – that's the biggest misconception. The best approach is to carry on as if I am anyone else, but just be aware that if I react in a way you wouldn't expect, it's reasonable to ask if I'm ok. I want to be treated like anybody else." D, an Indian male working in the software development industry

Are some of the bullet points above true for *some* people who have mental illness? Yes, but it truly depends on the person themselves, their personality, motivations and life experiences. The above descriptors are potentially more indicative of someone's character and how life has impacted them, and are not always specific to a mental illness diagnosis.

A lot of the above assumptions typically come from misinformation, lack of information, or single specific experiences that may be extrapolated to be wrongfully representative of many. Let's consider what this might look like.

If someone grew up with a parent who had a mental illness that the parent refused to acknowledge or deal with, this person may have witnessed a frustrating and chaotic version of mental illness during their formative years. This could easily color how they view others with mental illness.

Or perhaps someone had a co-worker who had depression, but in addition to that, wasn't a team player and struggled with personal accountability (separate from their depression). This person may have then drawn the parallel that the depression *caused* laziness around work tasks, when they were in fact unrelated. Perhaps someone heard several stories from different friends of theirs about people in their lives who "absolutely lost it" and vivid, subjective descriptions of what those breakdowns looked like.

R, who we heard from earlier about his depression (page 12), shared with me about how early in his career he chose not to talk about his mental health condition at work because the culture clearly showed that they would either bar people from advancement, or push them out entirely, if they showed any mental health issues. He recalled that his firm very clearly viewed mental health issues as a flaw and weakness.

There are innumerable ways that people arrive at assumptions – whether it's through lived experience, hearing stories, or what they've observed in isolated moments. The trouble is that when those assumptions go unchecked, they're then incorrectly and unfairly placed on others around them whose behaviors may "kind of" resemble something they once saw or heard… despite the fact that they're a wholly different person.

"Overall, it's something that's manageable. Even if it's heightened, I can still function and do my responsibilities at work. My experience and intelligence is on par with my co-workers." E, a Caucasian female working in the tourism industry

MENTAL ILLNESS CAN BE A STRENGTH

I want to take a moment to explore a possibility that you may not have considered: that certain mental health conditions may actually be a *strength* at work, where someone can channel their symptoms into incredibly productive, creative or helpful work.

Think about the resilience, tenacity and mental toughness required to manage ongoing mental health issues, manage your finances, relationships, succeed at work, and to deal with the challenges we face every day. Living with a mental illness takes serious self-awareness, courage, and insight, not to mention the vulnerability and openness required to address and work through issues that arise from it.

I've seen in my work that people who experience mental illness, are aware of and manage it, often have higher levels of empathy and compassion for others. They're aware of what intense emotional distress can feel like, and therefore typically want to be supportive to others in similar circumstances. I know leaders who have had long-standing mental health issues, which has made them more empathetic to their team members if they're going through a tough time.

Many impressively accomplished people have also had their own struggles with mental illness. Some of the most successful people I know have intense clinical anxiety, and their form of coping is by productively channeling it into their work. They remain passionate about their work, and impact their community in a positive way.

Below are a few high-profile people who have done just this, using their massive social platform as a way to contribute to changing the social narrative around mental illness:

- Catherine Zeta Jones: actress, has Bipolar II Disorder (also known as Cyclothymia).[9]
- Buzz Aldrin, the second man to walk on the moon, has struggled with addiction and clinical depression.[10]
- Jane Pauley, American TV news anchor and journalist, has Bipolar Disorder.[11]
- Lieutenant Général Roméo Antonius Dallaire, retired Canadian senator and human rights activist, has struggled with PTSD, depression and substance abuse.[12]
- Janet Jackson, award-winning singer, has clinical depression.[13]

"Mental illness hasn't impacted my work because I've never let it. For me, there are times where it's a real struggle, but I'm so stubborn that I won't give into it. It's one of the things that's made me as good as I am at my work. I always asked myself what I could do better, so that helped me to push through. It's only me that notices, no one else notices, in terms of my work output." R, a Caucasian male lawyer

THE CHALLENGES: HOW MENTAL HEALTH CAN NEGATIVELY IMPACT WORK

While there are positive ways to view mental health and mental illness in the context of work, it is also important to acknowledge when the impact can be negative and what that manifestation can look like.

Although challenges will be unique to each person and their life experience, there are some general themes to be aware of, further proving the point that this is absolutely a workplace issue. As our mental health influences the building blocks of how we view ourselves, how we interact with others, and our environment, this can impact how we view and do our work – particularly if we are in one of the valleys instead of atop a peak.

When someone is struggling with their mental health or has a diagnosed mental health condition that can have "flare-ups" or consistent symptoms like other chronic physical illnesses, this can sometimes impact how we show up, how we feel about, and do, our work. Unlike the unhelpful, stereotypical list on page 22, the following list are some manifestations that can occur, as signs of emotional struggle.

Emotional challenges:
- Concern about others viewing them differently due to their behavior changes
- Difficulty concentrating or prioritizing tasks
- Lowered motivation (particularly prevalent with depression, due to low mood)
- A negative or self-critical mindset
- An inability to work: going off on sickness absence or short/long-term disability for mental health issues (particularly if caused by chronic unmanaged stress or being overworked)

Behavioral challenges:
- Reduced overall engagement
- Disconnection from role purpose or work peers
- Changes in communication pattern (withdrawing, irritability, change in conflict style, etc.)
- Absenteeism (disengagement from work as a form of self-care, self-protection, or managing mental bandwidth)

This truncated list offers some insight into what's potentially going on with someone, and what drives some of that behavior when flare-ups occur, or if someone has trouble managing a chronic mental health condition. And some people may be struggling and hide it very well, so you wouldn't even notice. But, just because these occur *does not mean* that they are lazy, weak, or not a valuable contributor to their company and society.

"Right after I wake up, I have to make a conscious decision to proceed. Good days, I can have good interpersonal conversations with friends and colleagues and end the evening pleasantly. On bad days, there's anger, confusion, inability to focus and lethargy." F, a Caucasian male working in the software industry who has Generalized Anxiety Disorder and Major Depressive Disorder

"When my anxiety is really bad, I have a hard time seeing anything positive in the day. Then I go into a spiral. I tell myself I'm useless, then it turns into a negative outlook where I can't do what I intended to do. I'm paralyzed by fear or panic. I'm incapacitated to the point where I can't do anything because my body is thinking I'm in mortal danger. It does pass, but there's not much I can do but ride it out." E, a Caucasian female working in the tourism industry who has panic attacks, mild depression and Generalized Anxiety Disorder

---

TIP

Looking beyond the impact on work itself, I believe that bringing the conversation around mental health into the workplace (where most of us spend the majority of our time) in an authentic, supportive way can make a huge difference to those experiencing mental illness or chronic stress. To me, there is no negative to this conversation, unless people don't know how to navigate that conversation. But, that's what this book is for.

As we covered earlier, there are many people who channel their mental health struggles into their work, almost as a way of using that energy in a different way and redirecting their focus so they don't feel the emotional distress as intensely or feel hampered by it.

In the next chapter, we'll take a look at where we've come from on the social journey around mental health and mental illness, leading up to the evolution of conversations in the workplace.

TASK
Learning and Connecting

This task asks you to begin having conversations outside of work about mental health to deepen your understanding. Its intention is to help you to learn something from someone's unique story that you wouldn't have otherwise known unless you had that conversation.

- Think of one person you know that you have a good relationship with that you know struggles with their mental health – be it a diagnosed condition or not. Make sure this is someone that you know outside of work (we will address this within the context of work relationships in later chapters).

- Ask them whether they would feel comfortable discussing their mental health with you. Gain their permission before continuing.

- Explain that you're "seeking to understand"; that your sole purpose is to learn and become more informed about mental health and different mental illnesses.

- Pick the right time and place for this conversation, where you're one-on-one and there is enough time to have a non-rushed conversation. In person, or at least via video, is preferable as this is a delicate topic and viewing body language is important.

- Questions to ask:
  - What is their experience of mental health? Do they have a specific condition?
  - What does it feel like specifically, day to day?
  - Does their mental health impact them at work? If so, how?
  - Ask, listen, absorb and learn. Most importantly, thank them for being willing to share that information with you.

Take a mental note of the new perspective you learned about this person, mental health, mental illness, and how that may have differed from what you may have assumed before. Look back on the task in Chapter 1 (page 16) – has this conversation reversed any preconceptions you had?

CHAPTER SUMMARY

- Mental health and mental illness cannot be compartmentalized, and therefore *are* workplace issues.
- Mental illness does not make someone weak or unproductive; mental illness can be a strength.
- Mental health struggles or mental illness can negatively impact work – and that's why conversations and connection to resources are so important.
- By acknowledging that mental health is a workplace issue, we create opportunities to help people when they need it.

3

WHERE WE HAVE COME FROM AND WHERE WE ARE NOW

Stories, perceptions, and opinions all come from somewhere. So, to look at where we are now socially, and at work, we must first look very briefly at where we came from.

WHERE WE HAVE COME FROM

A BRIEF HISTORY OF MENTAL ILLNESS AND MENTAL HEALTH

The references to mental health in general, and mental illness in particular, have been around for millennia. Dr. Ingrid Farreres created a helpful chronological depiction of the history of mental illness, tracing it as far back as 6500 BC. She highlighted that depictions, explanations and treatments of mental illness were used as a way of marginalizing people as "the other", making sense of their "misunderstood" behavior, with repeating cycles throughout the years.[14]

Throughout the centuries, people with mental illness were frequently depicted as being unhealthy and defective. They were also assumed to be demonically possessed or evil, as religion (and not scientific evaluation) provided the sole explanations for the unknown.

These old theories drove the creation and usage of extreme medical "treatments" that were barbaric and untested – with the purpose of trying to "cure" someone of "abnormal behavior". Interventions over the centuries included methods such as exorcisms, directing a powerful fire hose at the patient, the unregulated treatment usage of cocaine, and other intense approaches not based in science or empathy. It was an iterative trial and error process, that did not take patient feedback into account. As Dr. Farreres explains, "Instilling fear was believed to be the best way to restore a disordered mind to reason."[15]

It wasn't until the 18th and 19th centuries that advocates began challenging the way people with mental illness were treated, focusing on moral purposeful treatment and treating individuals with dignity and specific mental health institutions.

In the 1950s the concept of talk therapies developed. Traumatic experiences, genetic inheritance, and brain damage were also recognized as potential causes of some forms of mental illness, and regulated trial-tested psychopharmacologic medications, (e.g. antidepressants) were developed.

The road to these developments was by no means easy and sadly negative stereotypes heavily steeped in history still hold true today in some circles and communities. I've witnessed these viewpoints in my work – both in clinical practice and in my organizational work. I still find that I need to teach people that having a mental illness doesn't mean that someone is defective.

As we covered in Chapter 1, mental health and mental illness are not the same thing, and the concept of mental health is much more shrouded in confusion for some.

The concept of "mental health" wasn't really formalized until the turn of the century. As society moved toward the empathic and humane treatment of mental illness, there was also movement toward the idea of a healthy state for the mind – which came to be known as the "mental hygiene movement".

Focus shifted to promote understanding and prevention. Attempts were made to understand the context of where behavior, cognitions and thoughts came from, whether that was from family, experiences, conditioning or biology. Psychologists, psychiatrists, mental health therapists, doctors, and social workers tried to understand the perspective of the individual as a whole, the importance of healthfully maintaining mental health "hygiene" and discovered how truly complex this was. Over time, the idea of mental hygiene slowly evolved into what we know as mental health today.

SLOW PROGRESS

Over the decades, we have seen growing trends of emotional health being discussed within families, and in our social systems of schools, universities, healthcare, and in governments all around the world.

Government organizations throughout the world (but most notably in Westernized countries like the US, UK, Australia, and some countries across Europe and Latin America) have made great strides to include the importance of mental health in their overall political agendas. Advocacy groups have done incredible work in representing family members, mental health and addiction providers, and other groups committed to strengthening access to mental healthcare.[16] Charities continue to research and promote positive mental health.[17] Psychologists have focused on research into emotion identification and the normalization of those discussions.

Through the bravery of many individuals and the trailblazing efforts of many company founders and others in professional seats of influence, there is a growing collective agreement that we need to promote discussions, shift culture, and change policy in the workplace around mental health. There is now an entire industry now solely dedicated to general mental wellbeing and a sub-set industry entirely dedicated to mental health at work (including yours truly).

There are mental health and mental illness international awareness days, weeks, and months littered throughout the year. There are even apps that are provided by employers for their employees to use around stress and mental health management, through reflection and cognitive-behavioral therapy techniques, and the like (as part of the wellbeing health benefits package).

However, while the normalization of discussions around mental health and mental illness have come on leaps and bounds, it'll be no surprise to you that there is still work to do. There is a rising demand that needs to be met.

Despite the fact that we understand mental health and mental illness far better now than we used to, sadly, our quality of mental health is diminishing and the rates of diagnosed mental illness are rising. This is due to a whole variety of factors, including:

- The trauma of experiencing the COVID-19 pandemic (more on this in Part 3)
- Chronic stress on the rise
- Chronic social media usage (which is linked to the development of mood disorders due to comparing ourselves to a falsely curated digital narrative of others)
- Constant access to technology
- Pressure to succeed at work

THE AWARENESS IS THERE – THE KNOWLEDGE IS NOT

While this progression is fantastic and commendable, awareness is not enough.

To create the change, to shift the conversation, people need to be shown *how* to have the conversation. Specifically, *what* to say.

What needs to be developed is the skillset of the language. Just as there's a science and art to diagnosis, there's an art to talking about mental health that comes with learning, practice and time. As a former clinical mental health therapist that now works solely on shifting conversations in workplaces, this book will give you the "how" that's adaptable for your work environment and won't shy away from the tough bits of the conversation.

MENTAL HEALTH BAND-AIDS

Awareness without understanding often leads to quick fixes, metaphorical mental health band-aids if you will: initiatives that look from the outside to be forward-thinking, but are really the easy option and still skirt the true issue. This might involve providing gym membership for your employees or championing the "positive mental health movement" (see page 36), all the while doing nothing to curtail the culture of wellbeing shaming or the psychologically unsafe work environment (see Chapter 5). As E explains:

"My company has recently noticed our high turnover rate. Instead of supporting the workers, they've instead put their efforts into further recruitment and HR benefits. Giving a $500 bonus for the health club. That's not what we need, but that's what they did. When people were complaining about their stress levels, and quitting, they just offered people free yoga classes – they could have offered vouchers for therapy. They don't broach the topic because it's hard. The easy solution is to offer money or something tangible. But that is not going to provide solutions."

LIMITATIONS TO PROGRESS

Despite the evolution that's occurred throughout the years, there is still misunderstanding, mishandling and miscategorization of the behavior of people when it comes to mental health and mental illness. This is apparent in society in general, and prolific in the workplace. And, these misunderstandings are the foundation of many roadblocks that make people nervous to talk about their mental health or mental illness at work. We'll explore a variety of these influential factors in Chapters 4 and 5, including culture, religion, and gender stereotypes around emotion to name a few. For now, I want to bring your attention to a few factors that have directly evolved from the history of mental health:

- Cultural perceptions (see page 58)
- Gender-based emotion stereotypes (see page 53)
- Generational differences – particularly around emotion, social norms and permissions (see page 83)
- Compartmentalization (see page 86)

WHERE WE ARE NOW

THE "POSITIVE" MENTAL HEALTH MOVEMENT

With a shift in narrative and a new awareness to navigate, there are usually differing opinions of how to get to the shared goal. The overwhelming majority of people in the mental wellbeing, and more specifically the mental health at work, industries have a benevolent goal in mind – to help people at work feel safe to speak up about mental health and mental illness, and to help people generally feel better so they can do good work.

However, an approach has popped up in the mental health at work movement that can be unfortunately very counterproductive: the encouragement of, and pressure to, maintain "positive mental health" all the time, *especially at work*. (Or in my world, "toxic positivity".)

Toxic positivity encourages you to take a positive outlook on a bad situation or experience *all the time*, regardless of the experience. It calls you to "always choose happiness" or "look for the positives". Programs, both inside and outside the workplace promise that you can have a "positive mindset in 90 days" and "#win at work". These programs are definitely popular – perhaps due to genuine interest, or with those seeking to avoid their uncomfortable emotions, or attended because someone told them to check it out (being volun-told).

In an interview for the *Washington Post*, Stephanie Preston, a professor of psychology at the University of Michigan who specializes in empathy, altruism and the way emotions affect behavior, hit the nail on the head when she highlighted some of the extrinsic reasons people may jump on the toxic positivity train at work: "It's an attractive behavior in people that makes them seem more well adapted and more popular with their peers, so there are a lot of reasons people want to seem or be positive."[18]

Sadly, this approach results in the minimization, denial, and invalidation of how someone truly feels. The positivity is a well-intended, encouraged method of coping, but how it lands is anything but that.

The programs that encourage "brain hacking for happiness" sadden me the most, telling the masses that they can formulaically get to happiness. This approach and curriculum don't take into account the broad scale of really hard experiences that some people go through, or the biology they inherited, some of which can be incredibly difficult to manage, let alone overcome. Those programs can marginalize people and may make them feel even worse as they fail at achieving what the program guarantees "if you really commit to it". It's all well and good if the creators of those programs were able to overcome their own struggles through channeling constant positivity, but each person has their own journey, and to give a one-size-fits-all promise just doesn't work.

As discussed in Chapter 1, feeling happy 100% of the time isn't what it really means to be human. We aren't meant to feel happy or positive all the time. Not even animals feel happy all the time. We have the ability to feel a whole host of emotions, some of which are negative, for a reason.

Imagine if someone has clinical depression, is struggling with addiction, going through a rough patch in their life, or is just having a crap day and just needs to get mad and cry. Now, add pressure on top that they need to be positive and push through it. What does that do to a person? Certainly nothing good. It leads people to deal with any negative emotions quietly on their own, because they're not part of the "positivity narrative".

If they buy in to this type of program outside of work, they may bring this "I have to be positive" mentality into work.

And when these programs are used at work as part of the mental health at work conversation, it's not helpful.

There has been a smorgasbord of research around this, the darker side of promoting toxic positivity. If this type of program is offered by a workplace, it's basically setting the tone for employees that there is the expectation that staff "keep it together". I've lost track of the number of speakers, programs, and initiatives I've seen who are purely dedicated to the maintenance of consistently "positive" mental health, and most destructively, an emphasis on maintaining positive mental health for productivity.

Unfortunately, these programs do what they're designed to do: influence workplace discussions – and in this case it's not positive – despite the title of the program.

Monica Torres, a reporter for *Huffington Post*, very aptly wrote that even though the positivity is well intended, that it's counterproductive and harmful. Torres interviewed organizational psychology professionals who echoed the sentiment that toxic positivity can create a work culture where employees can't share how they truly feel, legitimate negative emotions are dismissed, and trust between colleagues is eroded.[19] You can see why I'm not a fan – promoting feelings of worry or guilt around "not being positive enough" isn't the aim.

Is it helpful to promote positive thoughts such as fulfillment when trying to be productive? Absolutely. Is that always possible? No. Sometimes, you are where you are, and you try to be productive despite that.

Whether it's a team that depends on you, an important deadline, or whatever the individual reason – people try to push forward. What would be more helpful is a program (which are starting to appear, including from yours truly) that encourages people to realistically acknowledge where they are and use a few self-reflection and action-oriented measures to help them move forward, even if it's inch by inch.

WHAT TO DO IF YOU ENCOUNTER TOXIC POSITIVITY AT WORK

If you encounter toxic positivity from people at work, Elizabeth Derickson, a therapist for the online therapy provider TalkSpace, has some great ways to constructively deal with toxic positivity in the moment and embrace your emotions:

1. Identify and accept your emotions
2. Give yourself time to experience your emotions, without judgment
3. Have a good support network
4. Realize that people may use toxic positivity as a form of avoidance because they're uncomfortable with their own negative emotions
5. Don't compare yourself to others[20]

The more realistic approach and how we should be integrating the discussions of mental health and mental illness into the fabric of workplace culture is to acknowledge the shades of grey, that mental health conditions arise, and it's ok not to be ok at work. And, it's ok to *talk* about not being ok at work.

THE LANGUAGE WE USE

The language that we use helps to shape the reality we all share.

It helps to shape our attitudes in how we view the world, the meanings of what we say to others, and to ourselves. When thinking about how we should be talking about mental health at work, language is a *big deal*.

More specifically, the words we assign to what we are thinking or feeling are important. Naming something brings it to life. These proclamations don't exist in a vacuum. We share these names and words with others, thus influencing how they view naming their own thoughts, emotions, and experiences. Harold Brüssow, a Swiss research scientist, described the impact of naming and language very well when he wrote about the deeper meanings and history about the concept of "health".

"Naming is the first activity of human beings when trying to make order of things surrounding us. Words reflect the experience of many generations and words constitute a collective subconsciousness that determines still today our unexpressed thoughts and actions, more than we are aware of consciously."[21]

Words matter. The influence of those words matters, especially as we continue to name and shape the narrative around mental health and mental illness. It informs the perceptions we hold and the social rules that we create and experience around how and if we can discuss this topic. Before we go into the *actual* language and *how* to use it (in Part 2), we need to look at *why* the words we use are so powerful.

The Evolution of Mental Health Language

Think about how we talk about mental health today, the variety of terminology we have to name our emotions, feelings, thoughts, behaviors, and actions. We haven't always had these terms of expression. What we use now is an evolution of and reference to the original terminology created in a clinical setting, that was eventually adapted into larger societal usage.

This terminology is the product of the development of a specific nomenclature that was created and discussed by countless professionals in the fields of psychology, psychiatry, medicine and counselling. It also took the bravery of countless people to take chances and speak up about how they were feeling, hopeful that someone would understand and try to help them instead of judging and treating them differently.

It's no wonder that there is tension in the changing narrative around mental health between generations. Here's an example. Think about the word "triggered", which means that you've heard something or witnessed an event that reminds you of a previous trauma. Historically, this word didn't develop until it was clinically noted in the early 19th century and wasn't really used socially until the 1980s due to extensive research and work done around post-traumatic stress disorder (PTSD). Over the years, that word gave people a succinct way to identify the reactive emotions they're feeling by saying "I feel triggered".

Its usage is common these days, both socially and *at work* – you'll find it used in countless self-awareness training programs, that help professionals and leaders to gain insight on who they are personally and how that manifests professionally through their communication.

The now-mainstream use of the word "triggered" is an example of the possible evolution of the social narrative and social permission around the usage of mental health terminology. It also shows that using this terminology can spur conversations. This, ultimately, is what this book is about.

The Unintentional Co-opting of Language

Throughout time, people have co-opted and loosely used certain phrases sprouted from mental illness terminology to either explain how they're feeling or to place judgement on something that has happened, or how someone has acted that they may not understand fully.

I've encountered a *lot* of examples of this, but one particular situation has stayed with me. I was waiting at a package store to ship a parcel. I overheard a phone conversation of a woman who was attempting to be supportive to whomever she was speaking with. She said to the person on the phone, "I'm so confident you have PTSD from that argument." The argument she then described sounded more like an annoying disagreement, as opposed to other kinds of arguments that end in people's relationships disintegrating, someone getting physically hurt, or worse. I shook my head in disappointment. That woman, while obviously trying to be supportive to whomever she was speaking to, picked a diagnostic term to describe that person's irritation, and had no idea who may have been standing around to hear her conversation. It could have been any diagnosis; the impact would have been the same. What if someone had heard her who *actually had* PTSD and felt as though the woman's mention of it diminished its gravity, potentially making them feel like that term, which may mean a lot to them, is used as a casual throw-away mention by others?

Most of the time people aren't misusing language out of malice. That doesn't mean that some people don't intend to use it with intended guilt or shame, they absolutely do. For those who use their words as cutting barbs toward others, it's often because they don't understand what they're experiencing from that other person. Some people become uncomfortable if they encounter behaviors they don't understand or haven't seen before, so they may use this negative language toward others as a way to self-protect and distance themselves. Or even in some cases, to make themselves seem like the mental superior over the person they're singling out. Social shaming, sadly, still very alive and well.

Generally speaking, for those without malicious intention, people will co-opt and use certain phrases to highlight the intensity or gravity of what they're trying to say to someone. In cases where people speak out being uninformed, it is often because they have heard someone else using similar language. Or for humor – even if lightheartedly intended. Or even because they don't have a different way to explain how they're feeling, so they use a mental heuristic (e.g. a short-cut) to say it faster in a way that they think people will understand. We live in a fast-paced world where people communicate, both in person and digitally, at the speed of light. So, while I actively work not to fall into this habit myself, and teach others not to either, I intellectually understand why people do it.

Language Can Be Destructive

The reason that the unthoughtful use of language around mental health is so destructive is that it contributes to *why* people who have mental health conditions, or even chronic stress, are sometimes still afraid to speak up. They may fear how their experiences may be commented on, evaluated, or viewed, through the words of others.

What does this look like in practice? Some common phrasing floating around could look like:

- "*That's so mental.*"
- "*OMG, I'm so OCD!*"
- "*What a psycho.*"
- "*Doing these year-end reports makes me want to kill myself.*" (Jokes about suicide are some of the most harmful.)

If someone had a chronic physical health condition, people wouldn't be so quick to use statements referring to those conditions to explain how they're feeling or to explain others' behavior. You're less likely to hear things like:

- "That workout was really hard. I feel like I have congestive heart failure."
- "My stomach hurts like I have Crohn's disease."
- "I'm so out of shape, I'm breathing so hard, it feels like chronic-obstructive pulmonary disease."

You see my point. Language around mental health in general, and mental health conditions, seems more easily co-opted and improperly used because it's a complex and abstract topic.

There has been a variety of research in recent years that has focused on the co-opting and misuse of mental illness language in society, and how it sadly perpetuates the stigma around mental illness. GoodTherapy, an international database that helps people find mental health counselors and therapists, explored how commonly used stigmatizing phrases can have an impact on the continued social language usage about mental illness and continuing the stigma. Their research found that this usage creates unrealistic assumptions about people and has a shaming and minimizing impact on people with mental illness who overhear this improper usage of language. They documented the frustration people feel about the co-opting of mental illness language when society tends to be more careful not to make the same careless language mistakes when it comes to physical disabilities, or even ethnicity or religion.[22]

Our Response

There are some people who experience these moments of improper language usage and are brave enough to use it as a teachable moment, calmly explaining why that person may want to use an alternative way to explain how they feel, or even more importantly, to not assume why someone acted the way they did and use negative language to explain it. I appreciate those people so much.

Others, understandably, can feel offended by this improper usage and go on the offensive, which isn't typically a good way to get people onside with your cause. It's easy to get fired up – I get it. What we need is to educate, not lecture. In Part 2, we'll look further into what to say and not say when it comes to language choice when you approach conversations about mental health in the workplace.

Take a moment now to ask yourself whether you have regularly or occasionally co-opted language around mental illness before. It may be the habitual use of a term like "crazy" to describe a family member, or exaggeration of how you're feeling. Perhaps you use these terms about yourself or toward others. Think about how you might be able to change the way you describe or perceive how you feel or how you talk about others' behavior.

PEOPLE WANT TO TALK ABOUT THEIR MENTAL HEALTH

In addition to thinking about the language we use and the constructive ways to discuss mental health, the data shows that people *want* to have the discussion. In particular, many studies have shown that workers *want* to talk about their mental health at work, and the negative consequences of not being able to talk about it.

In particular, Mind Share Partners and Qualtrics conducted a study published by the *Harvard Business Review* in 2019 which found that the younger generations are overwhelmingly frustrated that mental health is still seen as taboo, and are reluctant to stay in organizations that don't talk about and prioritize mental health.[23]

The study also showed that mental health is the next evolution in diversity and inclusion, and that inclusion around mental health and mental illness is a vital discussion in the workplace.

Sadly, the data in this study reflects my earlier experiences when promoting mental health at work discussions in companies. The study found that nearly 60% of employees surveyed have never shared their mental health status at their companies, less than half felt mental health was a company priority, and even fewer saw their managers as mental health advocates.[24]

The discussion around mental health at work is shifting with each generation. While 86% of all respondents thought that a company's culture should support mental health, this percentage was even higher amongst the younger generations. The shift indicates that younger employees are hungry for their employers and leaders to normalize discussions about something that they were raised to see as healthy and reasonable to discuss.

Most notably, the study showed that younger generations will seek to work elsewhere if they don't feel safe to discuss mental health at work and can't get that reasonable need filled at their current company:

"Half of Millennials and 75% of Gen Zers had left roles in the past for mental health reasons, both voluntarily and involuntarily, compared with 34% of respondents overall — a finding that speaks to a generational shift in awareness. It is not surprising then that providing employees with the support they need improves not only engagement but also recruitment and retention, whereas doing nothing reinforces an outdated and damaging stigma."

Time magazine health journalist Mandy Oaklander echoed this sentiment in the data she found in her research for a piece she wrote.[25] She described how the younger generations of workers are becoming less willing to hide how they're feeling at work, because they feel they shouldn't have to.

It's fantastic that the data shows that the younger generation are taking action with their feet – leaving work environments that don't promote discussions around mental health. But, the reality for many is that they can't forego a steady salary just because their company doesn't support mental health at work. And while it's clear that younger generations see the mental health at work discussion as reasonable, the opposite viewpoint held by older generations drives major differences of opinion on the "appropriateness" of the discussion in the workplace. The Baby Boomer generation of workers (born 1946–1964) are far less comfortable discussing their mental health at work. The power of generational differences in the limitation to the progression of mental health at work is alive and well (see page 83).

The direction needed is clear. All employers will eventually need to turn their attention to mental health in the workplace. Social and generational change will push them to adapt in a purposeful way.

WHY WE NEED TO GET IT RIGHT

I want to end this chapter by emphasizing why it's so important to get this right. When people have challenged me in my work and asked, "How is mental health a workplace issue?" I always reply, "How could it not be?"

You'll find me coming back to this argument a lot in this book, but below I have set out three compelling reasons why we need to do the work, and change the culture around mental health at work *for good.*

FOR THE INDIVIDUAL

If the need to talk is there, and if employees can't leave a company, then they will stay, and suffer in silence. This could lead to an employee feeling less engaged, experiencing triggering episodes if they have a diagnosed mental health condition and increasing stress levels, feeling quiet or even overt resentment, harboring distrust and withdrawing from work relationships. They may go on sickness absence or short-term disability for mental health issues. They may be able to hold it together enough that they put a bandage on the proverbial wound, and just keep slowly bleeding. All of the above serve to show that we need to get it right for the individual.

MORAL OBLIGATION

We need to get it right because, frankly, it's the right thing to do. In a work environment that really gets it right, employees feel supported and connected to colleagues. Business owners have a moral duty to look after the wellbeing of staff, beyond just the bottom line. This benefits the employee personally and professionally with greater productivity and impact.

THE BUSINESS CASE

From a business perspective, the case is clear. Billions are lost due to poor mental health, sickness absence from work, lower productivity due to poor morale, downward spiraling engagement, and high attrition rates. The Mind Share Partners and Qualtrics study referenced above also highlighted the economic impact of 200 million lost days at work each year due to mental health conditions (equaling $16.8 billion in employee productivity).[26] The employer who does not set mental health as a business priority may see higher rates of absenteeism amongst their staff, disengagement from work, and potential conflict with peers or leaders.

Companies who normalize mental health discussions

↓

Appreciative employees

↓

A workforce that supports one another

↓

A company that succeeds together

Discussing mental health at work, and doing it really well, is no longer a "nice to have". It's a necessity.

TASK
Challenging Language and Assumptions

In this task we are going to tune in to identify language you hear others use and try to alter this usage in a gentle way. There are plenty of examples that occur around us all the time. With a deeper understanding of the power of language, and why we need to get it right, your ears may now perk up the next time you hear someone make a statement that you feel is continuing the stigma.

Remember – you're aiming to seek to understand, by asking questions and not criticizing. If you really want to create change around the narrative in a conversation, you need to get people onside.

For this task, use an outside-of-work one-on-one conversation with a friend or well-known acquaintance. Say you find this person making very clearly judgmental comments about a colleague's behavior from their company, or even about their own mental health (e.g. saying something judgmental about depression). They seem to attribute this behavior to a negative stigma around mental illness.

Your response could be: "We have no way of knowing what's going on for them behind closed doors. Let's reserve judgement and suspend assumptions. I'm sure we'd want that same courtesy for us, right?"

Or: "I'd like to understand – can I ask why you're saying it like that?"

By seeking to understand, you're giving that person a moment to stop and pause; to examine why they said what they said.

They may have been on autopilot. They may have used the wrong words. Or they may need their assumptions and perceptions checked.

The good thing about doing this one on one, is that person may be more likely to have that frank discussion because it's not happening in front of other people. You may be surprised by the constructive discussion that you have about uncovering unconscious bias and perceptions around mental illness, or discover that the person may have been using humor to subtly bring up their own stuff.

The next time you hear someone using phrases similar to those on page 43, seek to understand, seek to educate, and seek to change at least one mind. Start small.

CHAPTER SUMMARY

- Through the efforts of many advocates, organizations, researchers, and brave patients, we have gained an understanding of how to helpfully treat mental illness.
- We have seen a growing awareness around emotional health, but slow progress in some areas.
- We must be wary of the toxic positivity trend around mental health.
- The language we use is powerful – be mindful not to co-opt mental illness language.
- The majority of people want to discuss mental health at work.
- The moral and business case for discussing mental health at work is clear.

4

THE ROADBLOCKS TO PROGRESS OUTSIDE OF WORK

All we know in life are our experiences.

People who have had positive experiences around discussing mental health or mental health challenges will naturally be more willing to speak about mental health in a variety of contexts, and sometimes even at work. They have had first-hand knowledge of it "going well" from the network around them. So, they carry those beliefs with them through life and into a variety of contexts.

L had a unique story to share around this. She was raised by an incredible network of women in her community who taught her that discussing mental health is good and that showing care was not only normal, but encouraged. And, they stood by this ideology, despite the fact that it was counter to the social narrative of being Nigerian and raised in England.

"In Nigerian culture, mental health is taboo. But my mom had challenges in her life, which made her view the world in a different way. She cared about others and was empathetic and understanding. She made that care normal. She influenced how I view and talk about mental health and how open I am about it. What I experienced from my mom and my aunties was empathy, love, care, and understanding toward everybody around them." L, a Black female working in the consulting industry

What a positive experience. But sadly, that's not the world that everyone lives in. Stereotypes, experiences, and belief systems drive the perceptions people hold about mental health and mental illness and influence the fears they may have about discussing those things. These possible roadblocks are important to consider when we move on to think about how to approach discussions at work and when taking into account the whole context of who someone is.

These roadblocks can stem from both inside and outside of work. While there are many factors at play, let's first look at five big factors outside the workplace:

- Gender
- Culture, ethnicity and religion
- Family of origin (the family that raised you)
- Media influence
- Your self-concept and belief system (how you view yourself) and the impact of previous negative experiences

Please keep in mind that while discussing these themes, I would *never* aim to represent the opinions of an entire group of people. There are always differences of opinion, experiences and voices. I will draw on studies, widely represented data and stories, and make some thematic interpretations for the purpose of understanding how these factors may affect someone's willingness to discuss mental health.

GENDER

By gender, I mean the historical traditional gender assignments of male and female. While the concept of gender has and is continuing to evolve, and is not binary as it once was, historically speaking only, global society has placed socially constructed rules upon humans in two strict categories when it comes to gender. Rules that dictate what each gender is or is not allowed to do, think, or feel.

In recent years, the mental health impact of gender-based societal expectations has come to light, and we have discovered how these expectations impacted the men and women who were told to behave a certain way. Neither gender was exempt from this impact.

WOMEN AND GENDER-BASED EMOTION SHAMING

Historically, women have been labeled as the "emotional" gender. Victoria Brescoll from the Department of Organizational Behavior at Yale University argues that the belief that women are more emotional than men is one of the strongest gender stereotypes held in Western cultures.[27]

Since society first started discussing mental health on a larger scale, women have been medically stereotyped to be more naturally predisposed to having mental health conditions, and more prone to being dramatic and over-reacting. There was even a medical name for it: hysteria.

Dr. Farreras (who plotted the historical chronology of the mental illness discussed in Chapter 3) even cited how mental illness in women was thought to be: due to a "wandering uterus" in 1900 BC; because they were witches in the 13th century; and due to poor metabolism and disease in the 16th century.[28]

Now, it is accepted that while there is evidence that in some cases, women can have a higher predisposition to *certain* types of mood disorders, eating disorders or personality disorders, this doesn't mean that mental illness occurs more *frequently* in women than in men. Men and women both experience mental illness, and certain mental health conditions are more likely to show up in women, while others are more likely to show up in men. Reported data shows that women are more likely to *seek help* for their mental health conditions than men.

Even though a diagnosis of hysteria has since been disproven, it has left a historical scar. That stereotype of female hysteria seeped into society, and into families. It's a stereotype that still lingers today, affecting women both personally and professionally. This gender-based emotion shaming and marginalization does happen toward men too, so we'll look at both. To begin, we'll focus on how that plays out for women.

I have witnessed this gender-based emotion shaming in my work, where I have witnessed men labeling women as too emotional for experiencing reasonable reactions to objectively upsetting events. It was simply this: a woman demonstrated an intense emotion that they didn't understand and made them uncomfortable, so the reaction was to tell her she's being too emotional, to silence her.

It's no wonder that there are countless women who are hesitant to discuss their mental health at work, because they don't want to be wrongfully stereotyped. For fear of seeming "dramatic" or "too emotional" and, worst of all, to be painted like they can't "handle their job". This happens across all industries; however some of the typically more male-dominated industries such as engineering, construction, or transportation can present additional obstacles for women to navigate when it comes to discussing emotional health at work.

E told me about her concerns about being transparent about her emotional health at work as a woman. She echoed the sentiment of countless other women I've spoken to:

"It's hard as a woman to be in a professional setting with anxiety because sometimes people will blame your reactions on a simple difference of gender, instead of a mental health condition. As a female, I feel like I'm stereotyped as a woman to be overly emotional, and I

have an anxiety condition on top of it. I have to work hard to make sure that I'm received in an equal way with my co-workers." E, a Caucasian female working in the tourism industry

When women speak up about mental health struggles, or a mental health condition, the gender assignment of being female automatically means this honesty is far more likely to be viewed in a negative way, that our *biology* is always to blame. This not only makes the women who do speak up feel demeaned, but the misunderstanding of those feelings creates additional frustration and distress. Dr. Joel Young, Medical Director of the Rochester Center for Behavioral Medicine, wrote a piece about the social narrative around the biology of women and the influence toward mental illness. He states that the discrimination women experience around this ironically leads to higher levels of stress for women:

"It's easy to write off this epidemic of mental illness among women as the result of hormonal issues and genetic gender differences, or even to argue that women are simply more 'emotional' than men... Sadly, discrimination can increase women's exposure to stress."[29]

Despite the efforts toward debunking these stereotypes, women are still generally and wrongfully seen as "too sensitive" or easily affected by their environment and feelings. This couldn't be further from the truth. Being emotional, empathetic, and in touch with one's feelings and mental wellbeing is a massive strength, particularly in leadership. Some of the best world leaders and company CEOs are female. Sadly, for many women, speaking about their mental health at work still comes with a costly price tag: their professional reputation.

It would be easy (and careless) to assume that it is solely men that make women feel this way. That's not the case – women can be tough on each other too. Women are just as capable of unfairly labeling, disparaging, and criticizing other women's vocalizations around mental health – in particular, if they don't share the same feelings and perceptions. I've always called this "girl on girl crime".

THE MENTAL HEALTH IMPACT OF TOXIC MASCULINITY

While women are expected to be sensitive and to be ruled by their emotions, with men, it's quite the opposite.

Historically, men have been expected to be tough at all times and wear that toughness as a badge of honor. The Mental Health Foundation in the UK explains how, particularly in England, men have historically had an expectation placed on them that "masculinity" means being strong, stoic, dominant and in control. [30]

D, an Indian male who works in the software development industry, told me about his childhood and the gender expectations of strength that were placed on him from a very young age, even in the face of extreme loss:

> "Growing up, when my father passed away and I was the youngest child with two older sisters, I was told to step up and be the man. Men are notoriously bad at speaking about their emotions, or showing vulnerability, and it's something I've really struggled with. There's an element of shame. There's a preconception that being the man means you've got to be the supportive one, you've got to be the rock, and it was very difficult to show my vulnerable side to my wife or to anyone. I've now realized how silly that notion is." D

And often, it's men who place this expectation on each other. I've seen, personally and professionally, some men go so far as to taunt other men for talking about mental health struggles and use cruel derogatory language while they do it. The rhetoric of "manning up" (one of my least favorite gender stereotype phrases that exists) is damaging and pervasive. And, some women do this to men too, because they were raised to believe that narrative.

"With my gender, there is some bias against expressing vulnerability or perceived weakness, especially around depression or anxiety. It's the term 'man-up'. Put on your big boy pants. It implies a real man deals with his s**t. But you know what dealing with it is? Asking for help." F, a Caucasian male working in the software industry

These very real socially constructed mental barriers have horrible consequences on men. When I see mental health initiatives in companies, the majority of people I've seen speak up have been brave women, and occasionally, brave men. There are many men I've spoken to that still don't feel comfortable to speak up about mental health in a work setting, even with initiatives that encourage them to. Why? Because the private beliefs they hold about mental health for men don't give them the "permission" to do so, in *any* setting.

The most common fear I've heard in my work is that they're worried they'll be seen as weak or incapable. And the *last* place they want to be seen that way is *at work*. You think it's difficult for women to talk about mental health at work? Quadruple that difficulty for men.

In his work, Dr. Joel Young also highlights the effect of emotional labeling based on gender, and how different the disclosure of emotions might be for each gender:

"Men are often socialized not to share their emotions and to view emotional challenges as a form of weakness. A man who reports intense sadness might be asked about his lifestyle or told to see how he feels in two weeks. A woman is more likely to be told she's depressed."[31]

This emotional gender labeling encourages men to hide their mental health problems. The result? Not talking about it or reaching out for help. The impact? Unmanaged mental health problems and, in some cases, potentially suicide.

Our gender can have a very real impact on how we think we're *supposed to* feel about mental health. And in turn, if we feel we can talk about it at work without consequence or judgment. This is a big roadblock for many. Thankfully, the societally imposed mental shackles around gender and mental health are being challenged and redefined aggressively, and with purpose.

THE CONSEQUENCES ARE REAL

Social stereotypes can prevent men from speaking up and getting the care they need. A 2019 BBC article frighteningly highlighted that in the UK, suicide is the leading killer of men under the age of 45 and that there are similar trends in several other countries.[32] The data cited describes how, compared to women, men are three times more likely to die by suicide in Australia, 3.5 times more likely in the United States, and more than four times more likely in Russia and Argentina. And, further data included from the World Health Organization has indicated that nearly 40% of countries have more than 15 suicide deaths per 100,000 men; and only 1.5% of countries show a rate that high for women.

CULTURE, ETHNICITY AND RELIGION

Simply put, the culture you're raised in, the country you're from, how you identify (your ethnicity), and your religion can all be influential in how you view mental health and mental illness.

The purpose of this section is *not* to bolster stereotypes, but rather to make you pause and remember that culture, ethnicity, country of origin, or religion can impact people's perceived reality of mental health and mental illness. This in turn can impact how they may feel about talking about mental health at work, and who they may feel comfortable talking to.

Examining how every single culture and ethnic group addresses (or doesn't address) mental health and mental illness is not the core focus of this book, and I'm acutely aware of the complexity and nuance of these topics. Therefore, I've tried to draw upon pertinent resources data, to acknowledge the wider context, while making it purposeful. I'm *not* aiming to represent entire groups of people, but rather show thematic trends that have emerged over time and the importance of how these factors can impact people's views of reality, and therefore impact perceptions around mental health and mental illness.

As I wrote this section, my experiences as an expat abroad in England, Australia and South Korea came to mind. How my personal views and professional experiences around mental health and mental illness as an American were compared and contrasted to the host cultures I was living in. Each experience was educational in seeing how other cultures felt about and discussed (or didn't discuss) mental health.

My time in South Korea showed the biggest cultural differences around mental health. In my pre-psychology days circa 2008, I lived in South Korea to teach English to young students. In conversations with my South Korean work peers and locals I met socially, I learned that emotional health *wasn't* discussed. My experiences, echoed in the research I've since read about the social perceptions of mental health and mental illness in Asia, illustrated that emotional health was *private*. Because if you had "issues" it was seen as weakness and could bring shame to your family name – a *hugely* important cultural value in many Asian countries (particularly in South Korea, Japan, parts of India and China).

I remembered feeling horrified when I learned about the high rates of suicide amongst young people when they didn't get into university or if they lost their job. Driven to suicide by the shame they and their family felt about this "failure". At the time, none of the locals seemed fazed as they told me about it, almost as if they had grown accustomed to someone ending their own life because it was such a common occurrence. Since then, discussions around mental health have started to slowly progress in the past decade in different countries within Asia, but with some trepidation.

I cite this lived experience as an expat abroad to show how the culture you're raised in can really shape how you view mental health, mental health difficulties, and whether you feel you have the *permission* to speak about these topics.

CULTURE AND ETHNICITY

In my research and interviews around culture and ethnicity and how those can impact views of mental health and mental illness, three roadblock themes arose from culture and ethnic groups:

- Lack of acknowledgment and social permission
- Perceptions of weakness, driving individual feelings of shame
- Lack of access to education and funding

We'll look at some examples within each theme to illustrate these points. We'll take a highlight reel look at a few different parts of the world, and drill into experiences of a *few* ethnic groups. We'll be taking a similar approach to religion later in this chapter. Several books could be written on these three topics *alone* – hence the truncated overview.

Lack of Acknowledgment and Social Permission

In some parts of the world, the concept of mental health as we know it today either doesn't exist, or if it does, has its own specific lens through which it has developed.

The developments around mental illness, diagnosis and treatment largely took place in Westernized countries – including, but not limited to, the United States, Canada, Europe, Australia and New Zealand. And, these countries still pave the way today. These countries are where the de-stigmatization and normalization of discussing mental health and mental illness have been mostly occurring. In countries within Asia, parts of Africa, the Middle East, parts of South America, and elsewhere in the world, the discussions around mental health and mental illness are still evolving. These conversations range from treatment and suitable resources or shifting the social narrative, to questioning whether mental illness is even *recognized* as being legitimate.

> *"Even right now, mental health isn't even acknowledged in Indian culture. That's how I feel. I think cultural pressures can be difficult."* D, an Indian male working in the software development industry

K gave me a detailed account of the lack of social permission she felt to talk about mental health and mental illness in the Black community. She specifically shared about what it was like to grow up with a mixed background (Black and Caucasian) and how often those different parts of her identity were at odds with each other when it came to discussing mental health or mental illness. Permission from one, and not from the other.

> *"Culturally in the Black community, there are so many factors that aren't being addressed when it comes to mental health. There are a lot of people of color out there who don't have anyone to talk to because there isn't an open conversation*

that can be had comfortably." K, a mixed-background female (Black and Caucasian) working in administrative support

In Africa there has been a lack of development around language and naming when it comes to mental health – which shows the lack of acknowledgment. A well-known Kenyan humor writer, Ted Malanda, said it quite aptly in an article he wrote for *The Standard*, a Kenyan newspaper:

> "*I can't wrap my mind around the fact that depression is an illness… [But] it is such a non-issue that African languages never bothered to create a word for it.*"[33]

In Africa, there is a social, governmental, and advocacy acknowledgment that a *lot* of work needs to be done around mental health in shifting the social narrative, but also the need for resources. Organizations like SMART Africa and the Africa Mental Health Foundation are helping to lead this effort.

Reports have also come out of the United Arab Emirates (UAE) when it comes to the stigma surrounding discussions around mental health and mental illness. A 2019 article in *Arab News*, aptly titled "The hidden face of mental illness in the Middle East", highlighted that a large YouGov poll indicated that fewer than half of the survey respondents stated they would seek mental health care if they were experiencing psychological issues.[34] However, thankfully the narrative in the UAE is shifting and the paramount necessity to discuss mental health and mental illness has come to the forefront. The article highlighted:

> "*The Arab population is plagued by issues that are no different from any other population in the world: depression, anxiety, eating disorders, addiction, suicide, self-mutilation, post-traumatic disorders, mood disorders*

and so on... The difference now is that the Arab world is willing to admit the problem."[35]

Perceptions of Weakness Driving Feelings of Shame

"In some circles in the Black community, mental health is looked upon as a weakness. You'd be shunned and ostracized." K, a mixed-background female (Black and Caucasian) working in administrative support

The National Alliance for Mental Illness (NAMI) echoes K's sentiments in its research on cultural influences from the Black community around mental health and mental illness. Views on the topic are influenced by a lack of discussion and education, thus leading to false beliefs that a mental health condition is a "personal weakness". Ultimately, this leads to a reluctance in the community to discuss mental health problems or seek treatment due to the associated shame and stigma surrounding mental illness.[36]

A similar theme in the research is around how collectivistic cultures (focusing on the family and community first, the individual second) have a lot of pressure around self-managing emotional struggles, so as to not burden others.

In the Asian-American community, Ryann Tanap, a first-generation Filipina-American and daughter of two immigrants, wanted to go to therapy and wrote about her experiences seeking treatment. She spoke of her internal conflict; how her country of origin and culture were at odds in terms of how she sought help, from whom, and how difficult it was to reach out:

"There's an underlying fear... that getting mental health treatment means you're 'crazy'. If you admit that you need help for your mental health, parents and other family

members might experience shame. They may assume that
your condition is the result of poor parenting or a hereditary
flaw, and that you're broken because of them. Seeking
help from outside the immediate family also conflicts with
the... cultural value of interdependence. After all, why
would you pay to tell a stranger your problems when you
should be relying on the strength of your community?" [37]

In Ryann's piece, she noted that The Substance Abuse and
Mental Health Services Administration (SAMHSA) echoes her
sentiment, with research that highlighted significant cultural
pressures to be successful, and showing any signs of mental
health distress is deemed to be a weakness. Additionally,
particularly in the home setting, sharing your emotions too much
is seen as a burden on others, and being silent is actually seen
as a strength. Here, not only are conversations about mental
health not happening, but they're being actively avoided.

The World Bank has also reported on the feelings of shame
Latin American people have around seeking treatment, coupled
with a lack of understanding of what treatment involves.[38]

Lack of Education and Funding

In some parts of the world, the stigma around talking about
or seeking help for mental health issues is so ingrained that
people don't receive any education around the topic – from
anywhere. Therefore, people experience these distressing
feelings, thoughts, and behaviors in silence and don't get
access to the help they need.

According to The United Nations, as of 2017 Kenya only had
about 80 psychiatrists and 30 clinical psychologists, about 75%
of mentally ill South Africans had no access to psychiatric or
therapeutic care, Nigeria only had 130 psychiatrists in a country
of 174 million people, and Ghana had only three psychiatric
hospitals and about 20 psychiatrists.[39]

When we look at Latin America, opinions held on mental health and mental illness range broadly across the continent. Factors influencing the ability or willingness to discuss the subject include different levels of government funding, access to mental health resources (e.g. trained therapists), and other socioeconomic factors. The World Bank is pushing for mental health to be included on the development agenda of different Latin American countries, so leaders can be more aware of how poor mental health is impacting citizens, so targeted government education programs can help shift the social stigma.

BRAZIL BLAZING THE WAY

Brazil is a front runner in Latin America in the discussions around mental health. The Mental Health Innovation Network (MHIN) reported how the Brazilian government massively reformed their mental health system as early as the 1990s to decentralize mental health services by encouraging community services, primary care integration and social support programs. This positively resulted in a 58% reduction in inpatient hospitalizations and doubled federal funding for mental health dedicated to community-based care between 2002 and 2014.[40]

In summary, you may be standing on the same soil and working for the same company, but you are unique people from different lives, places and backgrounds. Honor, acknowledge and seek to understand those differences.

Pause.

Don't assume that someone's views and experiences around mental health and mental illness are the same as yours. These experiences and viewpoints that are held by people will be brought into the workplace. If someone grew up in a culture or community that didn't talk about mental health or mental illness, or even recognize it, Wellness Wednesday lunch-hour talks or pleas for employees to speak up about their mental health may be met with a hesitation or discomfort that has nothing to do with the workplace.

RELIGION

Think about the personal dilemma we have when deciding whether or not to talk about emotions based on our culture, family, or lived experiences – and add an existential layer of pressure and a potential evaluation from a deity on top.

Religion can be deeply personal for people and, for some, it can touch all aspects of their life – including how one might view mental health in general, the development of mental illness, and if they feel they can talk about it, and to whom.

To be clear, my point is *not* that religiosity has a poor impact on mental health and should be pulled away from the mental health discussion. Instead, I want to illustrate how religious upbringing can *influence* how we view mental health. And more importantly, how to be mindful of and understand the influence from someone's religious faith on their willingness or hesitancy to talk about mental health.

An article on religiosity and mental health in the Brazilian Journal of Psychiatry explained that while religion has positive benefits such as enhancing the resilience, personal peace and purpose, it can have a negative impact too – including high levels of guilt, doubt, anxiety, depression and enhanced self-criticism.[41]

My research around religion and its impact of views of mental health yielded the following themes:

- "Appropriateness" of who to seek help from
- Fear that mental illness means demonic possession, lack of faith, or distance from God
- Maintaining an "appearance" to your religious community

Who Can Advise You

Religion can influence who the "appropriate" parties are to seek help from when times are tough: that the religious community are the people to go to and the teachings and texts of the community will always have the "answer" to the problem.

Let's look at an example within the Russian Orthodox religion. Anton Ivanov, a mental health counselor of Russian descent, and Clifton Mitchell, a professor who specializes in overcoming challenges with therapy-resistant clients, wrote an article on the Russian Orthodox Church's influence around mental health. In particular, they highlighted that the depiction of a religious body as the "ones to trust" can be a very strong influence on people in the community about whom to seek counsel from when it comes to mental health problems:

"People still rely on the Russian Orthodox Church to 'solve' their issues. People go to the church to have all their questions answered by priests and in hopes of magically ridding themselves of their mental health issues by either drinking holy water or attending public worship. Russians view priests as authority figures and trust them much more so than they do mental health therapists."[42]

Unfortunately, while receiving support and having a support network from a religious community is positive, it doesn't always meet people's needs. Sometimes people need clinical mental health treatment that their religious community cannot provide, or may believe isn't necessary.

Possession, Sin, and Lack of Faith in God

Researchers Wesselmann and Graziano looked into religious beliefs around mental health stigma, and the depictions of mental illness being a "result" of being sinful or possessed. They found that as religious teachings depict the development of mental illness as being due to having a lack of faith or sinning, it can further stigmatize mental illness and discourage people from reaching out to get the care they need, from believing that the treatment is even helpful, or even talking about it with peers. [43]

A piece published by Rutgers University about religion and mental health, particularly in the Latinx community, highlighted that these skewed religious beliefs about mental illness make people believe they need to deal with mental illness solely through prayer, and so they don't reach out for help. This adds to the burden they bear quietly, and potentially contributes to higher rates of suicide in the community.[44]

E shared with me what it was like to grow up Roman Catholic and the clear messaging she received from her religious community about her mental health struggles: that praying will help her and that she developed her "issues" to begin with because she strayed from being close to God. Her religion never gave any other parameters. She recalls:

"I'll never forget that after putting up a blog post about my panic attacks, I had people from my old church community messaging me. They told me, 'You need to come back to the Lord. You need to get closer to Jesus, that's what's wrong with you.' The worst part of it is they meant well. Everyone was so nice and saying they were praying for me, but also that, 'You have got to heal with us and with the church, because that's why you're sad, you're so far from G-d right now.'" E, a Caucasian female working in the tourism industry

Keeping Up Appearances

F shared with me how mental health and mental illness were viewed in the Jewish community he was raised in. As I'm also Jewish, hearing perspectives from another Jewish person from a Jewish community in another city, from a different life, was very interesting. Similarly to the other collectivistic cultures referenced earlier, there was a large pressure not to "embarrass the family", despite the fact that what he was experiencing was very normal.

"In Ashkenazi Jewish culture, especially in the more religious communities, we are expected to present a carefully manicured exterior to the members of our synagogue or youth group, and that includes hiding elements of yourself that could be perceived as embarrassing. It may not be embarrassing to you, but it's embarrassing to your parents or grandparents' generations. So, it's passed down that you should feel shame about it." F, a Caucasian male working in the software industry

These are a few poignant examples of the narrative that exists for some around religion, mental health and mental illness. My point here is to encourage you to pause to seek to understand and acknowledge potential differences (not to be prescriptive).

The above research, data, social trends, and stories about culture, ethnicity, and religion provide us with a *mere glimpse* into the complex social systems that can impact someone's view on mental health and mental illness, from the context of their individual background. And, the views they may bring with them into work.

Now let's have a look at familial influence on discussions around mental health and mental illness: the messages we receive in our formative years.

FAMILY OF ORIGIN

For many, the word "family" brings up painful emotions; for others it's a positive topic; and for others, it's a wholly dissociated topic that doesn't elicit emotions at all. And for most, it's a mixed bag.

The family unit is an ecosystem. Conversation rules within families are core to that ecosystem – whether conscious or unconscious. And certain things are prioritized over others (like success and status over wellbeing).

This applies to the comfort or discomfort around discussing mental health and mental illness. And, if the leaders (parents) of this family ecosystem did not receive "permission" to discuss these topics in their family, or it wasn't a priority, and kept those beliefs into their own parenthood, it could prove difficult for them to give their own children the permission to discuss it.

If certain individuals push the boundaries and challenge other family members to talk about something they aren't comfortable with, it can stress or fracture the system (or in more positive cases, push the system to adapt and evolve). If someone can't get the information they need from the family system, or the "ok" to discuss these topics, they may:

1. Continue to believe that these rules permeate into larger social systems (e.g. friendships, work, etc.), and view the topic as taboo.
2. Seek education and validation from sources outside the family system to understand their own feelings and experiences. This ultimately fosters their growth around understanding mental health and mental illness. They receive "re-parenting around emotional education" elsewhere.
3. Receive a nudge from outside the family system from others who are signaling to them that it's ok to open up, and then it becomes a slow-drip of re-education, self-discovery, and speaking up.

With this in mind, the family system either gives or deprives us of permission to speak up about mental health and mental illness. How mental health and mental illness are treated or spoken about can be carried from childhood into adolescence and adulthood – and, ultimately, into work. It doesn't mean that we can't change those opinions, but the impressions take time to remold.

Instead of delving into family therapy theory here, I want to draw upon lived experience – unique stories that bring the concepts above to life.

P, a Caucasian female who works in the medical industry, shared with me that family members in her extended family that were a bit "different" were labeled as "crazy": "It was simple: you're either ok, or you're crazy." She spoke of how her parents, who were first-generation Americans that immigrated from Europe, had a limited understanding of mental illness, and therefore it wasn't part of the *allowable family narrative*.

F described how his family system was forced to address the topics around mental health and mental illness as his sibling was struggling with behavioral issues and was later diagnosed with a mental health condition. This experience ultimately led his parents to broach the topic with him, to discuss this development within the family and why his sibling would act certain ways. Ultimately this led to F being given "permission" to talk about his own struggles within the family and seek treatment, so he could start naming and understanding how he felt and how to constructively deal with his emotional struggles.

> *"My sibling having a diagnosable condition created a platform from which we could have a discussion. As such, as a teenager I was diagnosed with Major Depressive Disorder and Generalized Anxiety Disorder, and it allowed me to receive the treatment I needed."* F, a Caucasian male working in the software industry

D spoke of a family narrative which solely focused on achievement and succeeding. He explained that the focus on education and achievement was so strong, and that when he did mention he wasn't feeling well emotionally, his family didn't listen. They would often be critical, comparing him to others:

"I couldn't tell my parents anything. It was a factual relationship, and I was to do what was expected of me. I found it difficult to talk about my struggles with them. Having that door opened earlier would have really helped." D, an Indian male working in the software development industry

K described what sounded like an expectation to maintain toxic positivity (as we discussed on page 36): if it wasn't positive, or at a minimum neutral, she was expected to keep it to herself. Her family system used positivity and neutrality to maintain its homeostasis and straying from that meant discomfort and disruption.

"In my family, openly expressing emotions that weren't happy or neutral was frowned upon. Any other emotion was swept under the rug." K, a mixed-background female (Black and Caucasian) working in administrative support

In summary, familial rules and boundaries can influence the permission we feel we have or don't have to talk about mental health and mental illness. And we bring these beliefs into work: if you were raised in a family where it wasn't ok to talk about mental health even to them, or it was discouraged from being brought up to others (and you associate it with feelings of guilt and shame), it's logical that you may not feel comfortable to bring up this topic with a manager or co-worker. This may be the perspective of people you work alongside.

MEDIA INFLUENCE

Whether it's television, movies, social media, radio or the news, the impact of media on our collective psyche is real and significant. For years, these information sources have informed us of developing social issues and trends. By its very nature, this commentary is filtered through a specific lens that may not take into account all angles. It's managed by humans after all. And often, this is to the detriment of the conversation around mental health.

That's not to say there's a nefarious intention to manipulate and sway (although in some cases, there is). Often, the problem arises when those disseminating the information, stories, or entertainment only scratch the surface of complex topics, and present that information through their own lens, that's colored by their own experiences.

THE NEWS – IF IT BLEEDS IT LEADS

Historically, when it came to the news, mental illness was typically only mentioned when it came to a violent crime or in questioning a prominent person's behavior. Dr. Naveed Saleh, physician and medical journalist, describes that, *"media portrayals of those with mental illness often skew toward either stigmatization or trivialization."* In Chapter 1, we discussed the importance of *not* generalizing around mental health conditions and separating the person from the illness. Sadly, historically the media has not achieved this, often showing the person with mental illness as disruptive to society, and that the illness dictates the entirety of who they are. Dr. Saleh noted that, *"Perhaps most concerning of all, the media often portrays mental illness as being untreatable or unrecoverable."*[45]

On a positive note, news outlets have been recently shining a light on the importance of discussing mental health. This narrative shift has been noticeable, due to the colossal mental health impact of COVID-19 – opening up important conversations about discussing how we feel (we'll take a deeper look at this in Part 3). Mental health professionals and advocates have even been regular contributors on the news to shed further light around the topic. Popular celebrities and athletes have been doing television advertisements for online therapy platforms. This is progress. But it will be years before the previous archetype is erased altogether from the media.

ENTERTAINMENT – TO PIQUE INTEREST, NOT TO DEPICT REALITY

The focus in entertainment is keeping viewers or listeners engaged, riveted, and curious... at all costs. Even when that cost means only presenting part of a topic and leaving out essential nuances. Northwestern Medicine published an article highlighting the unhelpful and inaccurate depiction of mental illness in pop culture, citing that:

> "The truth is, not all depictions of mental health in the media are healthy. In fact, many TV shows and films have an alarmingly poor grasp on what it really means to have a mental illness and perpetuate harmful stereotypes that feed the stigmas attached to it."[46]

The trouble with only presenting part of the story is that this presentation of mental health can influence people's beliefs on mental illness and lead people to hold polarized and incomplete opinions. Thus, a mental shortcut is born for when people encounter others whose behavior they don't understand.

Typically, entertainment hasn't show instances of high functioning mental illness because it's not as entertaining. And when they do, it's depicted as someone who's so anxious that they're lightspeed workers on the verge of a breakdown, usually in a comedy. It doesn't tend to show someone sitting at home crying the whole night with a crippling depressive episode, and then leading a company-wide meeting the next day with 200 people.

The good news is that high functioning mental illness, and general realistic mental health struggles, are starting to appear in some TV and films, slowly but surely. Think *Silver Linings*

THE ROADBLOCKS TO PROGRESS OUTSIDE OF WORK

Playbook (depicting the main character with Bipolar Disorder and how he navigates medication, therapy, and a new romantic relationship) or *It's Kind of a Funny Story* (depicting a character who goes into inpatient psych treatment for suicidal thoughts and follows the struggles he has and the relationships he fosters while there) or *28 Days* (depicting addiction and struggles in rehab). In recent years there's even been the inclusion of mental health trigger warnings at the beginning or end of TV shows, meant to warn viewers of upsetting events that may occur in the episode like suicide, rape or domestic violence.

Yet when you have fictional hit movies like *One Hour Photo*, *The Joker* and *Girl, Interrupted* that show the much more intense side of mental illness, it's easy for people to be influenced to think that those with mental illness are all inherently violent and unstable. Even though the stories are fictional, they are *based on real* illnesses – which can impact people's perceptions of those real illnesses.

If we think about the cultures where mental health isn't discussed and education is not prioritized, depictions of mental health in the media can be an extraordinarily harmful, misleading influence.

The Association of Industrial Psychiatry of India published a research article that examined the effects of media on mental health perceptions in India. The research highlighted that as people in India are constantly using new platforms of media technology, but don't have the familial and social experience of discussing mental health and mental illness, they tend to look to the media for guidance on these topics. Unfortunately, its portrayal of mental illness to a broad audience that hasn't had a larger societal discussion has left a negative and unrepresentative mark on the topic:

"The media contribute to mental illness stigma through the exaggerated, inaccurate, and comical images they

use to portray persons with psychiatric disorders as well as providing incorrect information about mental illness... Unfortunately, the media consistently portrays persons with mental illness as violent, murderous, unpredictable and have themselves to blame for their condition... This has resulted in the belief in the general population that persons with psychiatric disorders are uncontrollable and dangerous and should be feared and avoided. Research has shown that negative views of individuals with mental illness are directly proportional to the time spent in watching television." [47]

YOUR SELF-CONCEPT AND PREVIOUS NEGATIVE EXPERIENCES

YOUR SELF-CONCEPT

Popularized by psychologist Carl Rogers in the mid-20th century, the term "self-concept" describes the self-constructed identity we create, the beliefs we hold about ourselves, and how others respond to us. Effectively, it's the big question of "who am I?"

Rogers believed that in order for someone to grow in a positive way and for their self-concept to flourish, their environment needs to provide the conditions of: genuineness (openness and self-disclosure), acceptance (being treated with unconditional positive regard), and empathy (being listened to and understood).[48] If these conditions aren't met during one's formative years, the odds of someone's self-concept progressing on a positive path are less likely. In practice, instead of "I am a strong person", it could become "I am weak."

The experiences we have throughout life and the people we encounter have an influence on molding who we are and how we see ourselves. Our personality, family, school, hobbies, jobs, friendships, romantic relationships, the groups we're a part of, how we interact with society. All of these have influence on our self-concept. This is not a static process.

Growing up with a wonderful support network, L's story provides us with an example of a positive self-concept. She had an environment of openness, acceptance, love and empathy, which made her feel more secure and have a positive association around speaking up when it came to her emotional health. In practice, this would sound something like: "It's healthy to talk about my emotions."

Alternatively, if someone's influences result in a negative self-concept, it may make them less likely to feel secure or safe to speak up about their mental health struggles. Given the potentially self-critical nature they may have of themselves, they may believe speaking up makes them weak, an outsider, or strange. They may fear this negative evaluation from others, which would layer on to the negative evaluation they may hold about themselves.

D shared that he was aware that his personal belief system he brought into work influenced why he didn't initially share about his mental health there. He was concerned to share because he felt he would be showing weakness, because he perceived having a mental illness to be a weakness. He was concerned that his colleagues may discount his opinions, thinking they were "tainted" by his emotional struggles – and that he wouldn't be suitable for advancement opportunities because he "couldn't cope".

If someone has a negative self-concept or a self-limiting belief system and aren't even remotely considering talking about mental health outside of work, bringing it up at work may not even be up for consideration.

THE IMPACT OF PREVIOUS NEGATIVE EXPERIENCES

As we just discussed, our belief system and self-concept can be majorly impacted by experiences that didn't go so well. Negative moments are etched into our brains, and when recalled on purpose or not, remind us of embarrassment, anger or sadness.

When it comes to experiences of sharing around mental health or mental illness, these can be particularly sensitive. To open up at your most vulnerable and be greeted with criticism, jokes, discrimination or dismissiveness would take its toll on anyone. This negative response would understandably drive us to not want to do it again. It's negative reinforcement.

The time and trust it takes to rebuild after an experience like this is significant, and, I'll be honest, some people never get there. But, many people do. Just because they've had bad experiences doesn't mean they can't have good experiences. We'll go over how you can be part of that in Part 2.

Now that we've covered some of the main influences outside of work for why people may be hesitant to speak up about mental health and mental illness, we'll turn to look at reasons that stem from inside the workplace.

TASK
Reflect On Your Own Outside-of-Work Barriers

This one is a big ask. You'll need to dig deep into the long and short-term memories that you hold about the factors discussed in this chapter that influence your comfort level around discussing mental health and mental illness. Please approach this task with honesty and without judgment. Consider the following reflection questions:

- Do any of the influences mentioned in this chapter impact how you feel about discussing mental health and mental illness? Do any of these influences make you feel like you can't bring these topics up in your personal life? If so, why?

- Did your family discuss mental health or mental illness when you grew up? If yes, how? If no, why not? Does your family experience make you feel like you can't discuss these topics with other people?
- Self-concept: how do you describe yourself when it comes to your mental health, or if you have a mental illness? Does your belief system allow you to feel like you can talk about this with other people?
- Have you had misunderstandings with people at work about mental health or mental illness who have a different background than you? How did you both react in that moment?

Once you have considered the above, work on shifting your mindset. Are there any beliefs you've adopted from these life influences that you want to change? Which belief do you want to update and how do you want to define the new one?

CHAPTER SUMMARY

- All we know in life are our experiences and what we're exposed to. We carry those beliefs through life and into a variety of contexts – including work.
- Many factors influence our comfort or discomfort around discussing mental health and mental illness outside of work, including but not limited to: gender, culture, ethnicity, religion, family of origin, the media, our self-concept and belief system, and previous negative experiences of sharing.
- Honor, acknowledge and seek to understand these differences. Don't assume that someone's views and experiences around mental health and mental illness are the same as yours.

5

THE ROADBLOCKS TO PROGRESS AT WORK

In this chapter we'll look at factors within the workplace that could be detrimental to conversations about mental health at work. These aren't an exhaustive list, but they're prevalent and impactful enough to be mentioned.

Here are some of the factors that stop people discussing mental health openly at work:

1. **Work relationships** with managers, leaders or colleagues who are: unsupportive, distant, or uncomfortable discussing mental health.
2. **Generational differences**
3. **Compartmentalization** which stops individuals bringing their whole selves to work.
4. **Psychologically unsafe work cultures**, where colleagues are judged, treated differently, prevented from advancement, bullied, or potentially fired for speaking about mental health struggles or mental illness.
5. **A culture of wellbeing shaming**, when people tease others for trying to strike a work/life balance to maintain their mental health.
6. **Leadership stoicism** – a belief that being a leader in the workplace means you can't discuss your own mental health.

7. **Good intentions**, but lack of resources to support the conversations (company-wide).

8. **The under-acknowledgement** of the impact of racial inequality and COVID-19 on mental health at work (which we'll look at in Part 3)

WORK RELATIONSHIPS

Whether we're conscious of it or not, we all have individual needs and expectations that we hope to have met from our work relationships, particularly from our team or manager. When those needs or expectations aren't met, or you encounter peers or a manager who don't show basic care or consideration toward you, it's not likely to make you want to open up to them. This could be a big blow if your outside-of-work life has already conditioned you not to speak up about those topics (as discussed in Chapter 4).

In practice, these relationships might:

- Be unsupportive:
  - o Your colleagues, manager or other leaders may feel (and have stated) that mental health is not a workplace issue.
  - o You may have been a part of, or overheard, discussions amongst your peers or leaders that talking about negative emotions, mental health, or mental illness show weakness or unreliability, and that this topic isn't meant for a "professional setting" (whatever their interpretation of this abstract concept is). This one is very personally driven and influenced by many of the factors in Chapter 4, from family and religion to past experiences.
- Feel interpersonally distant:
  - o You asked your manager or colleague to speak with you about some struggles you're having, and they

either haven't gotten back to you, or keep putting off the conversation.

- Show discomfort discussing mental health:
  - o Your manager may have mishandled an employee mental health situation in the past, so now they actively avoid talking about mental health.
  - o It's too "complex", so leaders and managers err on the safe side, and avoid discussing it with their teams.

While the above is wholly undesirable, it's important to remember that each person that acts this way will have their reasons. They could be struggling with their own mental health, their own discomfort around discussing mental health stemming from their upbringing, or pressures from elsewhere in the business that you aren't aware of.

This in *no way* excuses their behavior, but they are potential factors to keep in mind when evaluating work relationships. Despite the anger or disappointment you may feel when encountering these situations, try to seek to understand *why* they may have done those things.

M, a Black female who works in the retail industry, recalls the painful, unsupportive nature of her manager when she was signed off of work for mental health reasons: *"I had emails from my manager saying, 'I don't think there's anything wrong with you. I think you're making this up,' completely invalidating my feelings. They didn't care."*

E described the "old school", distant nature of her colleagues when it came to discussing mental health at the office. *"I fear being 'othered' if I speak about my mental health with my coworkers, because we do not cultivate an environment at my job that's understanding of differences. We don't address mental health whatsoever."* She felt there was no drive or desire to dig deeper about the staff's mental health needs.

J, a Caucasian female and army veteran, observed that while mental health *seemed* supported in her last role, she felt it was just lip service – all talk and no action.

The effects reach beyond individual relationships. If a leader or employee of a company holds negative biases and assumptions about mental health, their infectious influence can trickle into the work culture. The very necessary challenge, therefore, is to change those preconceived notions – changing the conversations, and ultimately changing the relationships at the root. If unchecked, those unsupportive, distant, and uncomfortable relationships (especially if they are plentiful) will breed a psychologically unsafe workplace culture and determine the "rules" of what can and cannot be discussed.

GENERATIONAL DIFFERENCES IN THE WORLD OF WORK

In the context of mental health, generational differences include: differences in access to education about mental health, awareness and conditioning around language to describe feelings (as discussed on page 40), social discussion, and the workplace cultural readiness that breeds the social permission to discuss it. This is experienced differently by each individual, depending on when they were born, and their individual life experience (I would never aim to stereotype an entire generation).

Camilla Lewis, a health management consultant at Aon, describes the challenges that generational differences can present to companies when trying to address such a complex topic:

"One major challenge businesses face with an increasingly large workforce is the widening of the age demographic and differing attitudes toward mental health. For the first time in history, we are seeing five generations of employees in

the workforce which are socially segmented into different groups... Traditionalists & Silence (born 1925–1946), Baby Boomers (born 1946-1964), Generation X (born 1965–1981), Millennials (born 1982–1996), and Generation Z (born mid 90s–mid 00s)... As a result, employers are facing an enormous variance in attitudes toward work and mental health as a wider age demographic go to work."[49]

To look at our current generation, we must look at the several that preceded us.

If you have as many as five generations of people at the same time and in the same workplace, there are a lot of gaps to bridge. You have different generations bringing different perceptions, belief systems, permission, and language to the table of how they discuss mental health and mental illness (if they're even willing to discuss it). This can have a huge impact on how this topic is viewed, treated, and debated – especially in the workplace.

It makes logical sense why mental health wasn't talked about at work historically. For a long time, many people didn't understand what mental health was, and definitely not mental illness, or have the permission to talk about "those feelings" in their personal lives. So, what would make older generations in the workplace think they could talk to their manager about it unless it had been spoken about at home in their formative years? It's no wonder that in 1950 that those conversations either didn't happen at all, or if they did, it may have been with great hesitation.

Crossing the Divide

There is an opportunity to achieve mutual understanding that crosses the generational divide, if we create moments to have those discussions with a mindset that's open to learning.

In Part 2 when we go over the *how* in detail, we'll cover some helpful conversational tips geared toward facilitating mutual understanding about generationally based definitions and opinions about mental health and mental illness at work.

TASK
Understanding Generational Differences

Think of someone you know personally that is of a different generation, at least 10 years older or younger than you. Ask to speak with them to explore your different ideas around mental health and mental illness. Follow the general guidance in the task on page 28 for the logistics of the conversation.

Make it clear that you're seeking to understand what it was like for them in comparison to what it was like for you.

With your questions, try not to make this person feel judged for their age, but rather, emphasize that you're seeking their perspective, and would like to share yours.

Questions to ask:

- How was mental health and mental illness spoken about to you when you were growing up and early in your career?
- Did those experiences shape what you believe about mental health and mental illness now, especially talking about it at work?

Share your experience, and that you want to discuss any similarities and differences, with the aim of finding common ground and bridging the gap.

If you have the opportunity to also have this conversation with someone from an older generation (if your first conversation was with someone younger), please take it! You will broaden your understanding considerably.

COMPARTMENTALIZATION

In Chapter 2 we discussed the fact that mental health is undoubtedly a workplace issue. But reticence to accept this remains, and a good chunk of the workforce are still keen to compartmentalize work and life.

When it comes to the separations we make now between home and work, it's more geared toward personal boundaries and the reasons we choose to keep those "worlds" separate, whether internally or externally motivated. It could be based on one's comfort levels, or what they feel is acceptable to share with work peers. The thing is, if we're still compartmentalizing at work with the purpose of hiding what's personally going on with us, it's literally defeating the purpose of normalizing mental health discussions at work.

PSYCHOLOGICALLY UNSAFE WORKPLACE CULTURES

Your work culture, intentionally or not, determines the unsaid rules that we need to play by around the disclosures of mental health or mental illness at work.

The workplace is really just an adult playground. We're all older, but it's very much the same. We all have a common space we're in (whether it's physical or virtual), relationships to maintain, toys to share, a king or queen of the jungle gym, and people who don't play nicely with others. When we think about this in the context of work, all of these affect the psychological safety we feel at work, and feed into our comfort or discomfort to share about mental health at work.

L described her experience at a startup where she experienced a psychologically unsafe culture: *"I wouldn't have felt safe telling people in that business that I had anxiety and depression because I was grieving my mother passing. I felt so let down by the business and didn't feel safe to speak up because there wasn't a culture to do that."*

Project Aristotle, a Google project that listed the top five things that make teams successful unsurprisingly found that the number one factor was psychological safety.[50] Harvard Professor Amy Edmonson clearly defines psychological safety in a context of work as: *"A belief that one will not be punished or humiliated for speaking up with ideas, questions, concerns or mistakes."*

The remaining factors that Google's Project Aristotle found were dependability, structure and clarity, meaning, and impact. These five factors all loosely touch on different elements of Maslow's Hierarchy of Needs (the needs we must have met to feel secure, safe and to move toward self-actualization/fulfilling our talents and potential). More on this in Part 2 (page 177).

To illustrate how the roadblock of an unsafe work culture may play out in the workplace, I want to draw upon the experiences of my interviewees. They told me how their experiences and observations of their peers and work environment informed whether or not they spoke up around mental health in general or if they had a mental health condition. The shocking descriptions of teasing, bullying and other unhelpful behaviors they mentioned having encountered are sadly quite common. I've heard of these behaviors not just from my interviewees, but from countless people in the companies I've consulted for, and from friends.

K and D shared with me some heartbreaking, cold examples of exactly what people *shouldn't do* that led them to feel very unsafe to speak about their mental health at work.

Aware that his behaviors were seeming "peculiar" to his team members, D told me about how he built up the courage to tell them about what was going on for him personally, to provide some clarity and context around the situation. *"I told them why I was acting the way I was so I could have peace of mind. The silence was broken. Some were understanding and offered to help. There were a couple of incidents that didn't go well."* Most frustratingly, D's line manager betrayed his trust and disclosed his mental health status to some team members without his consent. And what's worse is that when he confronted the line manager about it, the manager threw D's mental health status back at him – blaming his "anxiety". This destroyed any psychological safety and motivation that D felt to open up about mental health at work again for quite some time. *"Even now, I'm trying to come to terms with that. To have a negative response when you put yourself out there feels like a betrayal and it makes you close up".*

K's psychological safety at work was impacted through *direct* mental health shaming and bullying. This occurred in front of her co-workers by a team lead who often reviewed her work. *"She told me that I 'walked like a sad person, everything about me indicates that I am a sad person'. I said to her, 'I am depressed, I recognize that can be reflected in my gait, but I don't need you to throw it out to me'. I was being singled out for something that I knew I wasn't the only one struggling with. The people that witnessed it were silent."* Similarly to D, K's psychological safety was obliterated by someone in a position of authority in the business. More on the importance of creating trust and safety in teams, especially as a manager, in Part 2.

While our "playground" is now an office, our psychological safety to discuss certain things is determined by what we *experience* and *observe* around us. And with a psychologically unsafe work culture, there is very little hope for open conversation surrounding mental health.

THE MENTAL HEALTH IMPACT OF BULLYING AT WORK

A 2015 study by The Workplace Bullying and Trauma Institute (WBI) found that participants reported the following psychological impacts from workplace bullying: 52% experienced panic attacks, 80% experienced debilitating anxiety, 49% experienced a worsening of their clinical depression, 30% experienced PTSD-like symptoms and intense feelings of shame, guilt and overwhelming sense of injustice.[51]

Typically, when we hear about bullying at work, we feel bad for those who are sharing the story. We may tell them to stand up for themselves or to tell another person in a position of power to try to help them. While these actions are desirable, it's important to pause for a moment and consider the significant mental health impact that bullying can have. As someone who has personally experienced workplace bullying, I can tell you the mental health impact is real.

WELLBEING SHAMING

I define wellbeing shaming at work as the act of colleagues making fun – passive aggressively, or directly – of other colleagues for taking steps to maintain their mental health through work/life balance. (Which by the way, is a healthy adult practice.)

Wellbeing shaming often stems from a desire to maintain the company's status quo or cultural narrative. And in some cases, trying to one-up others. And it's infectious: when colleagues see others do it, they may think this is the way to "fit in", so start replicating that behavior toward others. The workplace playground dynamic continues.

I would venture to say that people who wellbeing shame may do so because they're quietly jealous, wishing they could give themselves the permission to do what the person whom they're making fun of is doing.

This may manifest as a quick conversational jab when someone takes their full time for a lunch break, voiced annoyance when someone is granted a flexible working request, or questioning someone's productivity if they choose not to sync their work emails up to their personal phone. Often it involves comparing tiredness and presenteeism levels, with the stance that if you're not exhausted by work, you're not working hard enough. This would sound something ridiculous like, "Oh stopping work at 3pm today? Must be nice to have an impromptu vacation."

Wellbeing shaming is a sign of the pressure to be constantly connected to work. A sign of the pressure to "win" (ugh) at work. This trend is not only unsustainable, it's dangerous. It's created an expectation where many people feel as though they can't disconnect from work, even when they really *need to* for emotional health reasons.

While the other roadblocks defined in this chapter have been about the *avoidance* of the mental health conversation, or the judgment of those discussions, wellbeing shaming is a totally different animal, occurring when someone sees the sprouting of mental health awareness and behaviors that follow. It acts to squash those efforts, and it's pretty powerful.

Shame is an incredibly powerful and destructive feeling to direct toward someone, particularly when it comes to health. A research paper by Luna Dolezal and Barry Lyons published in the

Medical Humanities journal focused on health-related shame, and if shame itself was a determinant of health. Their findings highlighted that not only is experiencing shame harmful to the person receiving it, but also to the relationship in which it's being used. Someone receiving shame can be made to feel like something is wrong with them, or worse, that they're inferior. It hits the core of their identity and can harm their self-concept and belief system.[52] (We covered this in detail on page 76.)

In a highly competitive job market and uncertain economy, it's understandable that many people are nervous to create a reasonable work/life integration that would go against a constant connection to work. Nervous to take a mental health day. Nervous to tell a boss that their depression is flaring up and they need to take some time to collect themselves. A lot of people still fear that discussing these things at work come with *very real* consequences.

In companies where people witness wellbeing shaming frequently, any movement toward conversation around mental health will eventually be silenced.

LEADERSHIP STOICISM AND THE MENTAL HEALTH SACRIFICE

Leadership stoicism – when managers are nervous to speak up about their mental health because they're in a leadership position – is an entrenched problem, whether self-imposed or stemming from a company culture that dictates "how a leader should behave".

Some managers may believe that to have these discussions wouldn't set a "good" leadership example. That a "good leader" is strong and doesn't crack. It's almost as if the leader has to become parental in nature – showing no weakness or fault, so as to seem steady and consistent for their team (a.k.a. their work children).

I've lost count of the number of leaders I've coached, who, in private with me, cried about how stressed they were. They felt they couldn't show this to anyone because they were worried of what others would think. When I looked at these leaders, I thought of the oxygen mask metaphor – that they needed to put their own on before assisting others. Yet, most of them felt they weren't allowed to. Reframing this stoic mindset is doable, but it takes serious work and a look at one's belief system.

Think about the additional pressures that leaders have: the need to be accountable for productivity, show value, and develop other people. It's ironic that these people, with so much responsibility on their shoulders, feel they aren't allowed to speak up when they're struggling. Leaders aren't immune to mental health issues – they're human like everyone else.

In an interview with the US Public Broadcasting Service (PBS), former energy sector CEO Philip Burguieres told of the countless leaders over the years who privately confessed to him about their depression, who felt they couldn't tell anyone because of the associated stigma around mental health and leadership. He estimated that 50% of CEOs, at some point in their lives, experience depression.[53]

Jason Saltzman, a CEO and entrepreneur, succinctly debunks the myth of the "flawless leader", and sharing about his own struggles as a leader [54]: "*I'm not a superhero. I don't have any superpowers. I'm a regular human being that goes through ups and downs like anyone else. But I'm also an entrepreneur and a CEO, which means people around me tend to put me in a category above themselves*". It's very true that historically people have looked to leaders to save them, to be "better" than the masses. Jason believes that, "*If we don't allow ourselves to be open and vulnerable, we're doing everyone around us a disservice*". It's exactly that – a disservice – a missed opportunity to show others that being a good leader also includes being a human who has their own stuff going on.

This expectation of stoicism is slowly changing. Many leaders have been brave enough to start speaking out about their own mental health struggles, stress, or diagnosed mental health conditions. Not only to humanize themselves as leaders, but also as a powerful form of role modeling: giving their team, employees and other leaders the permission that they can speak up too.

Chief Wellbeing Officer at Deloitte, Jen Fisher, explains the necessity of role modeling: *"The leader sets the tone for the organization... Lots of organizations have health and wellbeing programs, but if the leader isn't modeling the behavior, the workforce won't either."* [55] It's like the "follow the leader" game we used to play as kids... which we *still* subconsciously do as adults.

It is a true leadership strength to advocate for speaking up about mental health and mental illness. It takes true courage to be vulnerable.

Dennis Miller, CEO and coach, highlights the four lessons he learned while coping with depression and holding a position in the upper echelon of his company:[56]

- Depression isn't a character flaw
- It takes courage and strength to seek professional help
- Emotional health should be an ongoing investment
- Depression shouldn't derail success

The last time I checked, courage, strength, self-awareness and emotional intelligence were great qualities to have in a leader.

GOOD INTENTIONS, BUT LACKING RESOURCES

There are, of course, workplaces which don't have toxic work relationships or a noticeably unsafe work culture, but still struggle to create the aimed-for culture around mental health. This roadblock at work is more around logistics and practicalities, considering the resources and funding available, and touching on some HR and legal issues (and perceived concerns) that companies face.

Some companies may not know where to start – desiring to move forward but acutely aware that they don't want to say or do the wrong thing. I honestly have sympathy for these companies. There is a *lot* of information that's out there around how to approach mental health at work, so it can be overwhelming to know where to start.

Others may name a lack of funding and resources as the reasons why they haven't yet tackled this area within their organization, resulting in no mental health training, and a HR department that understandably doesn't have the time and bandwidth to add mental health initiatives onto their gargantuan list of tasks. They can't, and shouldn't have to be, everything to everybody.

> *"My company isn't set up to accommodate or deal with mental health concerns, requests, or initiatives. Our HR is focused on benefits and payroll. It's not focused on employee wellbeing. I doubt heavily whether our managers and senior managers have had any training on mental health response or awareness."* F, a Caucasian male working in the software industry

Some companies may be hesitant to discuss the topic because of potential legal concerns when opening up discussions around a complicated and sensitive area. Despite the existence of anti-discrimination laws around mental health, mental illness, or mental disability that were created to provide guidance on navigating these areas in the workplace – not everybody gets it right (hence the hesitation). For example, a lot of American companies have historically not discussed mental health or mental illness at work because:

- From the employer side, lawsuits happen quite easily in the US and companies are concerned about implied liability.
- From the employee side, there are not as many individual legal protections for workers in the US as there are in, let's say Europe, so individuals are more concerned with the consequences of speaking up because they fear losing their jobs.

The above scenarios are not insurmountable.

With the right intention and analysis, it's very possible for the leaders of companies to pinpoint the above issues as their roadblocks to creating a better mental health provision, and to then unpack why these barriers exist, and make an action plan of how to deal with them. More on this in Part 2 in *how* to actually tackle this process as a leader.

TASK
What Inside-of-Work Factors Are Stopping You From Discussing Mental Health at Work?

Reflect on your own fears and influences about why you are or aren't concerned to talk about mental health at work. Consider the following questions:

- Do these feelings stem from your current employer, or past employers, that you've carried with you?
- Did specific people at work influence you to feel this way? Who were they?
- Have you observed interactions between other colleagues at work that made you feel unsafe to share? What specifically did you observe?
- Can you identify opportunities at work where you wanted to share, but didn't, and why?

- If you've identified specific factors inside of work that make you feel hesitant to share about mental health, who would you want to raise this with and why? What are you hoping will come from this discussion? Highlight one key outcome you would strive for.

By clarifying these feelings, the source of where they came from, and who you want to speak with, this exercise will tee you up to have the conversation – after you learn about the language to use in Part 2.

TASK
Seek to Understand How Others Feel About Mental Health at Work

If you feel comfortable, speak to a colleague about why they may or may not feel comfortable about talking about mental health at work. This could be a good opportunity to sense-check with someone you're comfortable with at work about your own perceptions or fears around sharing about your own mental health. It's a good in-between step for before you speak up.

- Pick the right time and place and speak to someone you have good rapport with about why they do or don't feel comfortable talking about their mental health in the workplace. Seek to understand if it's personal or work-based reasons.
- Make sure you're very clear with them about why you're asking (e.g. you're seeking to understand how others feel about it). Reassure this person it's for educational reasons *only* and that you respect their privacy.

- Seek to understand, and if appropriate and you're comfortable, share your own reasons about why you may be hesitant to discuss mental health or mental illness at work. You may learn about the commonalities or differences you share despite being from different walks of life.

Keep in mind that this person has their own experiences, feelings, and journey around mental health or mental illness. So, while this information-seeking mission is useful, try to keep their comments in context. Because ultimately, you need to decide on what works best for you.

CHAPTER SUMMARY

- Distant or unsupportive work relationships, generational differences, compartmentalization, psychologically unsafe work cultures, and wellbeing shaming all influence people's comfort level to speak up about mental health at work.
- Leadership stoicism is a dangerous trend and unhelpful in the effort to create open workplace cultures. It is a strength for leaders to show vulnerability and courage as a role model in discussing mental health.
- Some companies have been held back by funding or have good intentions, but are uncertain/fearful of where to start.
- These are all solvable roadblocks, as long as there is willingness, empathy, and good intentions.

PART 1 CONCLUSION

We covered a lot of ground in Part 1. We've discussed the clear-cut case of *why* we need to discuss mental health at work, from the complex history of mental health and mental illness, to where we are now and what stands in our way. A myriad of reasons remain as to why some people are still rightfully nervous to discuss mental health at work. Personal reasons. Work reasons. All of which have an impact.

So, now we turn our attention to *how* to further the mental health narrative at work, and break down those roadblocks.

There are, of course, many ways to go about this change on a larger scale, that are impactful and needed: changing which individuals are placed in leadership positions, changes in company policy, company-wide communications, the inclusion of mental health benefits at work, company-wide training, and more.

But this book is not about those big shifts. This book is about how you, *as an individual* – whether you're an employee or a leader – can play your part in the change you hope to see.

The power of the individual was obvious throughout many of the roadblocks we discussed. An individual has the ability to take away someone's permission to discuss mental health; to play their part in creating an unsafe work culture; to be guilty of wellbeing shaming. We looked at many instances of an individual's negative influence.

In Part 2, we'll consider the *positive* influence an individual can have: the part you can play to create the ripples in the pond to create larger change. It's *your choice* if you want to have a negative or positive impact on mental health at work discussions.

We'll look at what it means to actually have mental health conversations at work and consider this from the perspective of different roles within an organization, namely:

- **The individual:** How to talk about your mental health at work if you are struggling, and do your part to reshape the narrative, inspiring peers and potentially even managers to do the same.
- **The colleague:** How to provide support as a colleague and have conversations with your peers. This is particularly valuable if someone feels they can't speak to their manager, and determines your impact on your work culture.
- **The manager or leader:** How to set the tone, provide support and discuss mental health with your team members. How to be the role model that we found could be so powerful in Part 1.

Additionally, we'll look at some really important considerations about mental health at work discussions, including the chaotic and uncertain times of COVID-19, and continued global racial injustice.

I'll continue to give you guidance and advice based on my own clinical and organizational experience, backed by research, and stories. Guidance that I believe in, that has worked for me, and that I'm confident will work for you.

Good leadership can come from anywhere, and leadership steers the conversation. Wherever you are in the hierarchy of your company, you can be a leader when it comes to championing mental health at work. Being a leader in this space is an opportunity to create, or redirect, a workplace culture toward valuing mental health.

No matter what your role, remember this: what you say, how you say it, and what you do *matters*.

Let's get started.

PART 2

THE HOW

6

HOW TO TALK ABOUT YOUR MENTAL HEALTH AT WORK

Before we jump into how to start conversations around mental health, and support colleagues or team members, we will first focus on how to talk about *your* own mental health at work. It is a two-sided conversation after all.

We're starting with the individual because how you share, and taking that first step to share, can be the catalyst needed to have that good conversation. One person's efforts of sharing their story can help shift the narrative – and inspire others to do the same.

You may be reading this from a place of struggle, wondering how to explain about your general mental health ups and downs, or your mental health condition, at work and ask for support. In this chapter, we'll concentrate on the best language and approach to take to open up about your own struggles at work and look at some issues you may encounter along the way.

It may be that you're reading this without a "mental health story to share" but a desire to be more open – ensuring you're contributing to and participating in the mental health conversation, with a vulnerability about the spectrum of emotions you naturally experience.

You don't need to be in crisis or have a diagnosed condition to share about mental health.

You may have experienced a tough event, be going through a rough patch, and just need some support. As we discussed in

Part 1, we're also trying to normalize discussions at work about the *full range* of emotions we all naturally experience as part of our mental health.

TIP

Important note: please *personalize* the guidance in this chapter based on what works for *you* in *your* work environment. How we talk about our mental health at work is a very personal and unique process. Take this guidance and use it in a way that *sounds natural* to you.

Often, *we* are our own biggest roadblock when attempting to start talking about mental health – held back by fear of shame, fear of the unknown, the desire to find a more acceptable "excuse" for our behavior because it's at work. Many of the roadblocks discussed in Chapters 4 and 5 may have resonated with you personally, and perhaps you've started unpacking the issues that you feel may be holding you back through some of the reflection exercises.

Whatever your personal roadblocks, I urge you now to give yourself permission to open up, to empower yourself to take the first step and to receive support from others if you need it.

We'll take this one step at a time through this chapter and consider six important factors:

1. Are you ready to talk about your mental health at work?
2. The role of personal accountability
3. What to do: the constructive approach (including who to talk to)
4. What *not* to do
5. How to respond if someone checks in to offer help
6. How to respond if the conversation doesn't go well

ARE YOU READY TO TALK ABOUT YOUR MENTAL HEALTH AT WORK?

If you feel ready to talk about your mental health at work, fantastic! You're about to take a massive step to help normalize this discussion at work. You are self-aware, brave, and willing to create change. If you haven't looked at it that way, I encourage you to do that starting today.

However, while this book is focused on *taking action* and talking about mental health at work, I want to make it crystal clear that if you're experiencing chronic stress, emotional upset or a mental health condition, you don't *have* to tell people at work. You are under no obligation to share this information, regardless of whether you are keen to progress the mental health conversation at work. That information is *your* information, and you can choose whether or not to share it.

You aren't failing at being an advocate if you choose to keep it to yourself. Perhaps you're going through a rough time and *do* want to share with your colleagues or boss, but don't have the words yet – that's ok too. There are many people who *want* to talk about their mental health, but can't organize their thoughts yet or may just need a more time.

Try to find a balance: while you don't need to rush this process, don't be afraid to give yourself a little nudge out of the nest. You wouldn't be reading this book if you weren't considering it.

TASK
Are You Ready To Discuss Your Mental Health At Work?

Pause for a moment and ask yourself:

- What are the specific things about your mental health that you want to share at work?

- Why do you want to share? What will it change for you at work by sharing this information?
- Who specifically do you want to share with and why?
- What do you want to get out of these conversations specifically (e.g. next steps)?
- When do you want to share?
- Do you have concerns about how these conversations will go? What are they and why do you feel this way? Are these concerns based on personal beliefs or something you observed at work?

I know that these are big questions, with big answers. And, answering these questions is easier said than done. But, they're necessary to work through because:

- Having clarity on the answers is crucial to having *constructive* mental health at work conversations.
- You want to be clear on *your why* and what you're trying to achieve (we'll cover this shortly).
- The answers may influence your perceptions or concerns about how your colleagues or boss may respond to you.
- Keep in mind that these answers may not come to you immediately. It may be an iterative process – deep self-reflection and awareness usually are.

We'll be exploring all of these questions and topics throughout this chapter. By the end of this chapter, you'll have fleshed out some of these reasons and made some decisions that will help guide you in this process.

THE ROLE OF PERSONAL ACCOUNTABILITY

Two of my favorite words: personal accountability. Simply put, it's being willing to answer to yourself for the resulting outcomes due to your behaviors, actions, and choices (or lack thereof).

You are an adult. With that comes the personal accountability for communicating to others around you about what you need and explaining who you are.

While the workplace has the responsibility of duty of care to its employees and to create a workplace culture that helps people to feel respected and safe, each individual also has a responsibility to self-advocate for their needs, share when something is up, and ask for help when needed. You are an independent being who makes your own choices. Speaking up, and how you speak up, is your choice.

It's important to grasp that while the *actual* impact you make is out of your control (your story will resonate with some and not with others; some will be ready to hear it, while others won't), what you *can* control and influence is the content of what you share, and whom you share this with. You can control how you encourage others to share and think about the impact you want to have. The questions you just went through in the previous task are some great questions to fuel the start of the personal accountability process – being concrete on what you want to do, how, and whom you want to share with.

WHAT TO DO: THE CONSTRUCTIVE APPROACH

When it comes to an actual conversation around your mental health, revisit your answers to the task on page 105. These answers will be your guide and show you the content that you want to talk about – both what you want to get across and your intentions behind it.

The "logistics" also matter: who you plan to talk to and when. You want to set yourself up for a constructive conversation that will be fruitful and hopefully produce your intended outcome. This may require some planning and strategy on your part.

That doesn't mean you need to control the whole process and make it 100% scripted. That's not how life, conversations, or people work – and would make for a really awkward conversation.

Think of the following points as your handrail to help keep your balance.

CHOOSE WHO TO TALK TO AND YOUR ANGLE

Be *intentional* about who you who want to share with and think about why you've chosen that person(s). Don't just share with anyone who will listen. Do you want to speak with a team member? Your boss? Your whole team? Whether you want to share with an individual, with your team, or in the company newsletter is up to you.

You need to consider *why* you're choosing that person, the desired outcome you want, and the approach you will take. This conversation may look different with different people. You may have a more casual approach with your peer whereas you may be more transactional or formal with your boss (depending on the rapport you have). Some things to consider:

TASK
Who Do You Want To Talk To About Your Mental Health?

Consider the following questions:

- What's your rapport like with the person you want to tell? What's the "vibe"?
- How would this person best "receive" what you want to tell them (e.g. are they fact-based, are they empathetic and respond to emotion-based words, do they prefer email or video to chat, etc.?)

- Within the context of the workplace relationship with this person, how can you describe to them why you chose *them* to speak to?
- If you want to share *with your boss*, what do you want to come out of that conversation? More on this one specifically shortly.
- If you want to share with your *immediate team*, what do you want to come out of that group conversation?

Having the conversation with different people at work will have different considerations. Think about how you can best approach that person. It won't work to speak to them as you would want to be spoken to – you need to plan to speak to them as *they* would best understand you. This will shape the kind of conversation that you have.

Below are a few introductory statements that set the tone, with different audiences. (*Please* make these sound like you, but you'll get the general sentiment.)

Speaking to a fact-oriented boss: *"I've been feeling really depressed and it's preventing me from focusing on my work. I need to speak with you because you're my manager, I want you to know what's going on, and I want to chat about how we could hopefully shift my workload a little in the next few weeks while I address this with my therapist and doctor."* Here, the focus is on how your mental health is affecting your work and productivity, with signposts to what you are doing practically.

Speaking to an emotion-oriented and empathic colleague: *"I'm feeling really stressed out and I feel like I have no one to talk to. I've always enjoyed working with you and I feel like you're a good listener – could we talk?"* Here, the focus is on your relationship and opening up about your feelings.

Speaking to your team (a collection of personalities): "*I realize that some of you may have noticed that I've been acting differently in the last couple of weeks. I wanted to let you know what's been going on just so I could give you all some context and set expectations.*" Here, the focus is on you acknowledging your place and impact within the wider team – while keeping them informed.

Once you've considered the task's questions, you'll feel a bit more prepared on who to speak with and how you want to go about it (having considered your audience) so you can have a *constructive* conversation about your mental health at work.

GET ON THEIR RADAR

Don't rely on signals or hints to let someone know you want to talk or need help. Not everyone is good at picking up on subtle clues, especially in an increasingly remote-working world. Additionally, if you work in a company where the culture is people being wary of "overstepping" into colleagues' personal lives, to expect them to know what's going on for your mental health without clear signposting is an unrealistic expectation.

When it comes to matters of the mind, be explicitly clear that you want to talk or need support. I've lost count of the number of times I've heard someone say, "*I really want to tell my boss, and I've hinted at it hoping they'd get it, but they haven't taken the bait.*" Or "*I tried to drop into conversation with a colleague that I had a really bad weekend mental health wise, but I don't think they got just how 'bad' I meant.*"

Think of all the stuff your colleague or boss has going on – their personal life, the 463 emails they receive every day, the pressure they receive from their boss, and the other team members they manage. They're also supposed to pick up on subtle cues from you on wanting to discuss your emotional distress or that you're not sleeping because of the 30% increase in your workload? Come on now.

Use your words and *create space* to say them by reaching out. Here's what this could sound like: *"I know you're really busy at the moment, but I need to have a quick catch up with you. Do you have 30 minutes later today to chat?"*

CHOOSE THE RIGHT TIME AND PLACE

As this is an important discussion, and if you know you'll need more than ten minutes for it, pick the right time and place to accommodate for this.

Depending on who you're speaking with, pick conditions that will set you and the other person up for success. This might be during a dedicated 1:1 weekly timeslot with your manager, or at the end of the day, or a slower day when your colleague seems to have some free time. Ask them when they'll have time to chat and explain why at a high level. What does this sound like?

To a colleague: *"When's the next time you're free for a chat? I have some stuff going on I was hoping to talk to you about."*

To your boss: *"I have some stuff going on that I was hoping to run by you. Can we discuss it in my next 1:1?"*

Naturally, many people might respond by asking, *"Sure, what's going on?"* Typically, the best thing to do following this on-the-spot question is to generally communicate that you have some personal things going on that you want to discuss and that you want to save it for a time and place that works for you both. The constructive response would be, *"It's some private stuff going on – I'd prefer to explain it later when we speak if that's ok?"*

Pick a time and place that works for both sides – you want it to be at a time where they have the actual time and (hopefully) mental bandwidth to hear you.

When it comes to choosing the right medium, Dr. Albert Mehrabian's research on non-verbal communication postulates that 55% of communication is body language, 38% is tone, and only 7% is through spoken word – meaning that *theoretically* 93% of communication is non-verbal.[57] So, in-person or video chat is the best, so you can see how someone is physically reacting to what you're sharing, beyond just what they're saying, as those can sometimes be in conflict with each other, and the body language is the *real* indicator of how they may be feeling. A phone call is a back-up method so you can at least hear the person's tone of voice – another big indicator.

When thinking about how you best communicate, and how that person will best receive what you're saying, it's important to remember that some people are more comfortable when chatting via synchronous communication (e.g. instant messaging) because it gives them time to think about their answers, questions, and organize what they want to say. Some also feel more comfortable in tough conversations when they aren't being "seen" by the other person. If you prefer this form of chatting, that's fine, but please make sure you are *very* intentional with what you're typing, consistently checking in with the person that they're understanding what you mean (even use emojis if you have to – you have more choices these days than you'll ever need).

If you're speaking in person at the office, make sure you're in a private space, or go for a walk outside if the weather suits. The main goal here is to have privacy and no distractions.

ESTABLISH CONFIDENTIALITY

The old saying, "If it goes without saying, you could say it was never said", is incredibly true. If what you're sharing with your colleague or manager is private, make sure they *know that*.

Make it *explicitly* clear and ensure they know your desire for confidentiality is about your needs and privacy, not that you think they'll be a gossip. This is important because you don't want to start off the conversation with making someone feel like you *don't* trust them. You want them to feel like you do, so they'll take what you're saying to heart.

A good way to say this might be, *"You're the first person I've talked to about this in our team. I'd really appreciate it if you kept this between us."* or *"I know we're pretty open about communication in our team, but please don't tell the other team members yet. I'm still deciding how or if I want to share with them, and I want to do that in my own time."*

Ensure you get verbal confirmation from them that they've understood your request. Making a request without checking in on how it's landed is a recipe for a misunderstanding.

HIGHLIGHT YOUR GOAL AND YOUR WHY

Be clear on why you're raising this with them, what you need, and what you *don't* need (refer to page 105 in the "Are You Ready To Discuss Your Mental Health At Work?" exercise you just completed).

Do you just need them to listen, or to take some sort of action – like helping to get you connected to the employee assistance program (EAP) or to muster up the courage to talk to your boss? Be clear on your purpose and what you're hoping to accomplish by sharing this information with this person.

Here's a few examples of what this could sound like:

- *"I'm telling you about this because I know I've been acting differently recently at work. I wanted you to hear directly from me about why I've been acting like this, so you didn't assume the wrong thing. And I wanted to mention a few things that would be super helpful for whenever we check in. Can I explain them?"*
- *"I'm really having a tough time right now. I don't think I'm ready to go to therapy – but don't we have an EAP? I feel like a quick phone chat with someone could be a good*

in-between step for me. Can you help me find out more about the program?"
- *"I'm feeling really overwhelmed. I don't want anything in particular; I'd just really appreciate if you could listen to me word-vomit what's been going on – is that ok?"*

Again, check in here and make sure you're both aligned on the purpose of the discussion so it can hopefully go smoothly. That they'll just listen, or help you brainstorm, depending on what you've asked for. The last thing you want is a steamrolling fixer if you just want a sympathetic ear. You need to be clear about which type of help you need.

EXPLAIN ANY CONCERNS

This will give you an opportunity to mention any concerns to the person and give them the opportunity to allay your fears. Make sure to use "I" statements and be specifically clear about your concern. Connect the "I" statement to the actual fear itself, or the outcome you're worried about (like the personal or workplace roadblocks we talked about in Chapters 4 and 5). This might be, *"I'm worried you'll judge me"*, or *"I don't want you to see me differently"*.

Hearing from the person that they won't see you differently, and when they mean it, is more comforting that we realize. So many people get stuck in their own head and perpetuate their fears and don't reality check these fears with those around them. Take the time for this step – divulge the fears – give the person the opportunity to put your mind at ease.

DON'T BE AFRAID TO GET EMOTIONAL

Crying, frustration and anger are displays of natural emotions. Resist the urge to apologize for experiencing those emotions or feelings, and just let them flow naturally. Don't flip a table or anything, but try to let yourself feel what you need to feel without second-guessing.

It's ok to be vulnerable. In Chapter 1 we talked about the *full* range of emotions that we experience naturally – that's what we're talking about here. It's ok to have emotions that don't feel good and to experience them in front of others. It's healthier to experience and move through this full range of emotions as opposed to denying their existence. By just sitting with these emotions, you're showing that they're healthy and there's nothing to be sorry for.

EXPAND AND EDUCATE

If someone doesn't understand how you're feeling, or doesn't seem to "get" your mental health struggle, educate them! If they're curious, it's a sign of empathy and trying to meet you where you're at. Give them the opportunity for this. Try starting with:

- *"What depression looks like for me is...X...Y...Z."*
- *"X influences how I look at..."*
- *"I know typically people with trauma may say they feel A, B or C, but for me it's been..."*

EXPLAIN CHANGES IN YOUR BODY LANGUAGE IF NECESSARY

You may be aware that you're not speaking as you normally would. You may be avoiding eye contact, shifting in your chair a lot, fiddling with a pen, or finding yourself turning away. If you're aware of yourself doing any of these, attempt to explain why, so the person doesn't think it's *them* who's making you writhe around like a noodle.

For example, if you don't want to make eye contact, explain that you're nervous, and that this is the first time you've talked about your mental health at work. Try: *"I know I look uncomfortable, it's because I am. I've never talked about this at work – so it's really weird and scary for me."* Or: *"I wasn't raised to talk about my feelings, so this is hard for me, but I feel like I need to, and I can't avoid it anymore. Looking right at you is making me nervous, so if my eyes shift as I talk, please don't think it's about you – it's just my own stuff."*

IF YOU'RE SHARING WITH A MANAGER

When it comes to your relationship with your manager, it's even more important to be clear on your *why*, your reasons for talking about your mental health.

If you're having specific concerns when sharing with a manager, make that *very* clear. Because that person sits in a position of authority, it's understandable that you might be concerned about what they think. That's ok – just create the space for them to know that and to confirm to you that your disclosure won't change anything. It could sound something like: *"I don't want you to think I can't do my job because I'm feeling this way. I absolutely can and want to do this job. I just wanted you to know what was going on for me since you're my manager and I want us to be able to work well together."*

A good manager will not only want to help you flourish in your role, but to also make you feel included, heard and supported in your team. If you're sharing with a manager, it's good for them to know what's going on for you, but also if there are specific next steps you feel you need. They should also be able to add to the list of possible solutions from their point of view.

Consider the following questions:

- Is it possible to swap projects with someone on your team?
- Do you want to include wellbeing check-ins occasionally during your 1:1s?
- Is your role so high stress that you want to talk about switching departments?
- Did you want your boss to be aware of changes in your mental health, so they could know how to best communicate with you?

Ask yourself these questions prior to going into the conversation so your manager can know what you'd like to accomplish by having that conversation.

TIP

When it comes to sharing with your manager, the points we discussed around confidentiality, highlighting your goal and allaying your concerns are all crucial. *Do not skip these.*

This could sound like: *"I know I'm valued, but I need to tell you that the workload I have is really triggering my anxiety. I don't feel good at work, and I'm not sleeping well at night. I don't want you to think I can't 'handle it', I can, I just think need some additional support. It would be really helpful to me if you could let me know that it's ok that I've told you this. I might need to talk to HR about getting a mental health accommodation and look at some of the company resources for more support. Can we talk about what that would look like?"*

IF YOU'RE SHARING WITH YOUR IMMEDIATE TEAM

You may be considering whether you want to share about your mental health more broadly with your team. You may want to consider who it would *help* to know what's going on for you, focus on your *why*, and your goal in sharing.

The breadth of sharing will be unique to the size and make-up of your company, your role, and will depend on your reasons for sharing. For example, if your goal is to explain some recent change in behavior, and within your role where you only interact with a few people, this indicates to you who you need to tell. If within your role you communicate with a variety of colleagues and managers across the business, any of whom may have noticed a behavior change, you may want to share more widely. It's up to you.

Some of the reasons you might want to share with your team may be:

- So everyone is aware of why you've "not seemed yourself lately".
- So they're just aware of what's going on, with no impetus to act.
- To ask them not to flood your inbox as usual with non-critical items that you have no direct impact on.

Logistically, picking the right time and place to share with your team is important too. Check with your line manager first about when the most useful time would be. Would it be at the end of a weekly team meeting? Do you want to send an email to your team members so you can construct your thoughts and they can reach out to you as needed? Also remember to mention any desired confidentiality.

Whether you choose to email, or bring this up in a team meeting, coming right out of the gate with the crucial information is helpful. This could sound like,

"I wanted to let you all know about something that's been going on for me. For those of you who've noticed that I've been acting differently, it's because of X. Some days I'm ok, other days are a struggle. I'd really appreciate it if you kept this within this group. I wanted to tell you all because we work closely together, and I wanted you to know what was up. I'd really appreciate in the coming weeks if you could please A, B, and C. If you want to chat with me 1:1, just let me know, but please understand I'm not ready to go into a lot of detail. Thanks for listening."

SHARING YOUR STORY COMPANY-WIDE

I have seen some *incredible* stories shared in the companies I've consulted and spoken for, where people have spoken about their experiences company-wide (live or recorded) and been met with appreciation, learning, and most importantly, others becoming inspired to do the same.

I remember a couple of sessions that I led in one company, where I purposefully asked if there was anyone who would be willing to share their story as part of my seminar. Several people volunteered. I remembered their colleagues' faces – some smiling, some crying – as people shared their stories. What stayed with me the most was the sheer number of unprompted stories that were shared, that were listened to, that were given space. The resulting change that happened in that company following those sessions was immense. I was so proud of these brave people.

So, if you want to share your story beyond the purposes of letting people know what's going on for you within your team, and you want to take more of an advocacy position around shifting the narrative in your company, this option is one to consider.

Deciding the *why*, your desired outcome, and *how* you want to do this are crucial. Remember, good leadership on this topic can come from anywhere, and it could come from you.

Make sure to take a lay of the land at your organization before embarking on this and look back at some of the roadblocks at work discussed in Chapter 5. Do any of these apply to your work?

Consider asking yourself the following questions:
- Are there certain beliefs or values about mental health (roadblocks) in your company that you want to help change through sharing your story?

- How do you want to do this?
- Has this topic been discussed at your company?
- Are a lot of colleagues complaining that they feel they can't talk about mental health, and you want to give them a voice?
- What avenue do you want to use? (The company newsletter? A post on the company-intranet? A recorded video that could be sent out?)
- Which leaders or people of influence could help you in getting out this message? Will your manager support you in this? Get the buy-in – leader sponsorship can be incredibly helpful.
- What research will you include? Your story is powerful and using data to back it up (to show you're not alone) can be the tipping point for some in believing the validity of the topic.
- What are the key points you want to share about your story? Make sure these pack a punch. People have very short attention spans – keep your story succinct and skip the rest.
- What desired outcome or action do you hope people will take?

If the decision makers in your company are looking for the business case around broaching this topic, I encourage you to share Why We Need To Get It Right in Chapter 3 (page 47) and the litany of resources available at the end. (And, to read this book!)

If your company hasn't yet broached the topic of mental health at work, that's ok. *Starting* the conversation is a great first step. It doesn't mean they have to create a full-on program straight away, but a willingness and curiosity to address the topic organization-wide in some shape or form is a start.

WHAT NOT TO DO

I don't want to be overwhelmingly prescriptive on what not to do. However, there are a few things that I would really recommend *not* doing if you want to share your story or are seeking to help a conversation go well, purely for the purposes of setting you up for success in those conversations.

DON'T ASSUME THEY'LL KNOW EXACTLY WHAT YOU MEAN

If someone doesn't know what Major Depressive Disorder or trauma is or doesn't know what it feels like to be so chronically stressed that you don't sleep at night, cut them some slack. If it's not something they've been exposed to, but are willing to learn, take the opportunity to educate them.

There's a balance to be struck here, when creating a teachable moment. Explain it in layman's terms as if it were the first time you were hearing it – and make sure not to be patronizing. But if they're curious, and it will aid the conversation, explain to them what it feels and looks like, how you experience it, and how it affects you in general and in a work context.

If someone seems a bit confused or unsure of what to say, tell them what would be helpful for you *at that moment*.

What would moments like this look like? Odds are, you'll be able to feel it.

The person you're talking to will potentially look uncomfortable, seem confused, respond to you in ways that kind of "miss the mark". If this happens, pause, clarify, and make sure you're aligned. Do this by using the powers of observation, and honestly, your intuition (e.g. your gut is telling you that something doesn't feel right). Using some of the same techniques used in counselling and coaching, this could sound like:

- Clarifying: *"I'm feeling like you're not understanding what I'm saying. Would it be helpful if I explain it in a different way?"*
- Directing: *"I can tell you want to help me, so let me tell you the best way how."*
- Addressing discomfort: *"I don't want to assume, but it seems like you're uncomfortable – is it ok that I'm sharing this with you?"*

Addressing discomfort in particular, while tough in the moment, can be *incredibly* helpful. It's basically calling out the larger issue at hand in an effort to break through that wall, gain mutual understanding, and move forward. In counselling it's called referring to the secondary process – these are areas that someone may not be aware of in the moment – but you're trying to create awareness for them. Addressing and removing these blocks is incredibly helpful in these conversations. (If you're in the supporter role, we'll look at how to use the calling out secondary processes as the supporter in the next chapter.)

By calling out those moments of tension, or misalignment, it allows you both to address it and move forward. Even though this is *not* a counselling or coaching conversation, the techniques are still incredibly helpful.

Remember to try to maintain awareness of potential generational differences in understanding around mental health and mental illness (e.g. if you're sharing with someone significantly older or younger than you are, see page 83). Aim to bridge the gap through shared understanding. This could sound like: *"I appreciate you telling me you don't know a lot about mental illness because you weren't exposed to very much in your life and haven't had a lot of these conversations, but let me explain what it means to me, if that's helpful."*

Even if there's a misunderstanding, it doesn't have to end poorly. Misunderstandings are opportunities to create shared understanding. Approach the process with the aim to explain, educate and to get on the same page. To do this, make sure that you're clear on your end.

DON'T ADD UNNECESSARY DETAIL TO THE CONVERSATION

Too much detail, especially non-essential details, will potentially cloud your ask or overwhelm and confuse who you're talking to. Not to mention, people's attention spans are becoming *alarmingly* short these days.

I'm not saying that you need to rush, but you need to be mindful and appreciative of people's time when they're dedicating it to you. Pick what they need to know (e.g. the big themes, the actions you want them to take, from your answers to the task on page 108) and leave the rest out.

Remember that your co-worker or boss *isn't* your therapist, doctor, parent or sibling. So, while it's great that they're willing to listen to you and be supportive, they're not a never-ending resource of empathy and time. Some family members and doctors aren't either, but you get my point.

Their role is to be supportive, ask about what you need, and depending on who you're talking with, get you connected to resources that can help you better than they ever could. So, your expectations – and how much you divulge – needs to be reasonable and appropriate in relation to this role. As your colleague, within the context of work, what do they need to know and why?

If you're supporting a colleague around *their* mental health, we'll go more deeply into being clear about the purpose of that role in the next chapter.

DON'T USE MENTAL HEALTH STRUGGLES AS AN EXCUSE FOR UNRELATED THINGS YOU HAVEN'T TAKEN RESPONSIBILITY FOR

Let me be clear: once you've told someone at work about your stress or mental health condition, don't use it as the reason that you missed a deadline, didn't complete a task, or to excuse a behavior if that stress or mental health condition was not the *real* reason. Not helpful.

If you want your mental health struggles or a condition to be taken seriously, and to constructively change the narrative around these topics, you need be clear about what it affects, what it doesn't, and when. A few (hard hitting) reflective questions to ask yourself to find these answers are:

- Are you just using X as an excuse so they'll cut you some slack and you can avoid consequences?
- Did you *really* not take care of Y because of your Z condition, or is it because you didn't manage your time properly?
- By using your mental health condition as the scapegoat, are you "crying wolf" and shifting the narrative around mental health in a way that isn't helpful to others?
- Are you leading this person to believe a false connection between your behavior and why you weren't accountable?

If you dropped the ball on a project, don't use that moment to share about your PTSD for the first time if it *actually* had nothing to do with it. If you want people to take mental health and mental illness seriously at work, don't give them a reason to think it's used as the fallback reason when things don't get done, or that it's used as an avoidance tactic.

DON'T ASSUME THAT THE OUTCOME WILL BE NEGATIVE

"You'd be surprised how many people do understand when you share your story. There's nothing wrong with telling your boss you have bad anxiety, and you need time and space to deal with it." E, a Caucasian female working in the tourism industry

I'm conscious that the fear that the conversation will go badly or someone will not care is *very* real for some people. And in some cases, this fear is not misplaced.

There *are* people who will react negatively, lack empathy and be uncomfortable talking about this stuff. There are *also* people who may be unfamiliar with the topic or not know what to say, particularly in a work context if they haven't discussed it there before, and it's possible these people may act a lot like the former.

If the *reaction* seems negative, that doesn't necessarily mean there will be a negative *outcome*. Give the person you're sharing with the opportunity to respond. This may require some open-mindedness and flexibility on your part.

Remember to be open about any concerns (see page 114) – address these head on. Use your "I" statements here. An example of this could be: *"I really want to talk to you about something going on for me, but I'm worried you won't care based on how this conversation started."* This gives them a chance to allay your concerns.

Also highlight your goal (see page 113) – what you want to get out of the conversation. If it was to change your working patterns or be referred to a company-provided wellbeing benefit, and you manage to achieve this within the conversation, the outcome was a success (regardless of the actual reaction, although having a caring reaction is desirable).

HOW TO REACT IF SOMEONE CHECKS IN WITH YOU

If someone initiates a check-in with you, asks how you're doing, or says they've observed that you don't seem like yourself and don't want to pry, then that's fantastic (maybe they've read the next chapter of this book).

Everything we've discussed so far – from what to do (page 107) to what not to do (page 121) all still applies. It's just that the *other person* has initiated the conversation.

One of the most important things you can do from the start is to *give them the permission to support you.*

It's common that when someone at work wants to ask a colleague or team member how their mental health is, they can feel somewhat nervous about overstepping boundaries or making someone feel uncomfortable. Reassure them that they're not being intrusive, that you appreciate the check-in, and let them know you want to have this conversation with them. Then follow the steps described from page 111 to establish the right time, place, establish confidentiality and make clear your ultimate goal. They just did some of the work for you!

IF YOU'RE NOT COMFORTABLE WITH WHO'S ASKING

If someone asks you about your mental health, and you don't feel comfortable with that particular person who's asking you, it's ok to draw boundaries and explain that you'd rather not discuss that topic, and thank them for asking you how you're doing. Remember, it's your story, your information, and you don't need to share it with every person who asks.

They don't need to know your reasons for not sharing, just that you don't want to. The clear way of saying this could be: *"I appreciate you checking in, that's really nice. I do have some personal stuff going on, but I don't really want to talk about it. If I change my mind, I'll reach out to you about it."*

If for some reason your colleague or boss feels offended because they heard you shared with someone else, be clear with the boundaries – they will survive. This could sound something like: *"Yes, I did share about X with Y, and while I appreciate you checking in, who I share about my life with is my decision. I hope you'll respect that. Again, thank you for asking and I appreciate your concern, but I'm asking that you respect my boundaries."*

While this may seem direct and even a bit standoffish, it's not. If you re-read that sentence carefully, there is nothing offensive or personally attacking about those words. It's a healthy adult boundary being drawn, clearly.

IF THEY ASK IN FRONT OF OTHERS, OR MESS UP

If someone asks about your mental health in a rude way, or in front of others, resist the urge to verbally skewer them. It's an opportunity to deal with the situation better than they did, with the aim to set boundaries, seek to understand why they did what they did, and craft a path forward. Let's look at how.

Choosing the right time and place to address this are important here, and you'll need to use your judgment if you want to speak with them privately or if you want to turn it into a teachable moment in front of others.

If you want to address it with them privately and not raise it in front of others in the moment, a private follow-up from you could sound something like: *"That wasn't the best venue to ask me about this. But now that you've asked, I am feeling stressed and I don't think that's anything to be ashamed about. I think some empathy or asking me in private would've been a better way for you to go about this. Help me understand why you chose to do that in front of our team."*

If you choose to address the person in front of others, remember, make it about destigmatizing mental health discussions (the larger issue at hand). This could sound like: *"Millions of people experience X issue and it's really common. Is there a reason you're singling me out and bringing this up in front of other people?"*

If they freeze and don't know what to do, they may have realized the error of their ways. In this moment, say something to diffuse the conversation: *"Let's move on. I know that joking about mental illness is something that a lot of people do, but maybe it shouldn't be. Hope you don't mind that I called that out."*

If they say something snide in return, keep calm and ask that the conversation move into a private setting: *"It sounds like we're not seeing eye to eye on this, so let's discuss this 1:1 later."*

While it may be uncomfortable for that person, they need to learn that mental health discussions need to be had in a constructive time and place and conducted with respect. It's a necessary lesson to learn and if they are unaware of what they were doing, then they need to gain some self-awareness.

If you can, use it as a teachable moment about why what they said or did is inflammatory and unhelpful. Find your own words for how to say that best knowing the context of your relationship with that person. Give feedback constructively, either in the moment, or the next time you're speaking 1:1. Use an "I" statement (page 114) to explain how they made you feel and show your perception of their approach toward you. There could be a good learning opportunity there and a moment for rapport building.

WHAT HAPPENS IF THE CONVERSATION DOESN'T GO WELL?

What happens if the person you're sharing with doesn't take your steer when you ask them to just listen and they go into "fix it" mode? Or you ask for help and they give you that deer-in-headlights look? Or, they're dismissive and even rude?

It's ok. Trust me when I say that there is growth and learning in discomfort here, for both of you. And your mission hasn't catastrophically failed. It may just mean that person may not be able to give you what you need.

TIP

This is an important lesson to learn in life, whether it's in or outside of work – learning and acknowledging what people can and cannot give you.

IF THERE'S A MISUNDERSTANDING OR THEY'RE UNCOMFORTABLE

Remember when we discussed calling out the secondary process (page 122)? That is your *strongest* tool to use here as the person sharing.

A key thing to remember here is that if someone is dismissive of what you disclose to them, they *may* have their own stuff going on that has *nothing* to do with you. Or they may feel uncomfortable discussing the topic for personal reasons, as we discussed in Chapter 4.

If they seem uncomfortable or uncertain of what to do, check in to see why they've reacted the way they did.

If they respond that they're just not used to the topic, or don't know how to help, then take it back to the basics: ask them just to be aware of what your needs are, to be compassionate if you are struggling, and to keep treating you the same way. You're not asking any more of them. Here's what this exchange might look like with a colleague:

Your colleague: *"I really don't know what to say here. Not sure where to take this."*

You: *"That's ok, I get it and I know it's not something you typically talk about at work. All I'm asking for is for you to be aware of what I've shared, that I need X, and to look at me no differently than anyone else. I'm still the same person, this is just part of what I'm dealing with. I'm trusting that this will stay between you and I – agreed?"*

Your colleague (hopefully): *"Alright, sounds clear to me, I think I can do that. If anything changes, just let me know."*

If your disclosure to a colleague or your boss is greeted with the good old suggestion to "be positive", take a deep breath and remember that they're most likely just trying to help. Let them know that, while you know they're trying to help, the encouragement to be positive isn't helpful. Be sincere and informative. This could sound like: *"I appreciate you want to make me feel better, but that's not what I need right now. I just need to tell you what's going on, and that while I do that, for it to be ok that I'm not feeling good."*

IF SOMEONE BETRAYS YOUR TRUST AND SHARES YOUR INFORMATION WITH OTHERS AT WORK

If someone betrays your confidence, don't crumble.

First of all, you shouldn't feel like you have something to hide. We're trying to bring discussions about mental health and mental illness out *into the open* at work. So please, remember that.

I'm conscious that people have varying degrees of what they want to share and who they want to share it with and when, but no matter what, there's no need to feel ashamed if someone else found out about something you shared to your colleague or boss that is *healthy* to discuss.

You didn't do anything wrong there, they did.

If someone else in your office informs you of this gossip out of concern, thank them for letting you know, ask them to respect your privacy and not share with anyone else. Tell them that you'll be addressing it with the person you shared with directly. And more importantly, own your story, normalize the topic, and don't act as if you have anything to be ashamed of – because you don't.

If the person who brought the information back to you is doing it to gain further gossip, there's a teachable moment there, reminding them that they're perpetuating the stigma and taboo. You could try saying: *"Thanks for letting me know. X wasn't supposed to share that with anyone because I shared it in confidence, but honestly, I'm not ashamed to have panic attacks because it's super common. I don't even think this is gossip worthy. Would this be as big a deal if I had hypertension or IBS? I don't think so. Anyway, I appreciate you letting me know so I can address it with them."*

As for the person who didn't respect your privacy, there's no need to go out on a witch hunt. Breathe – create the teachable moment. Use your "I" statements (see page 114).

Let them know the impact their actions have had and the boundaries they've crossed. Even though you can't control it, they'll hopefully learn from that experience. If they don't, then you've learned where your line is with that person.

Whether it's a colleague or your boss who has inappropriately shared your information, seek to understand *why* they did it – because you don't want to assume – and knowing the reason is important. Was it accidental? Were they gossiping and being malicious? Both are wrong, but knowing the motivation is important, and making sure you can address it, so it doesn't happen again.

Dealing with the situation *directly* is always desirable; working it out between the two of you. People are less likely to be defensive if you approach them privately as opposed to telling other people or reporting them straight to HR. Let's have a look at a couple of scenarios:

A Scenario with a Colleague

If your colleague has betrayed your trust, try to find the right *private* time and place to bring it up. Whether you choose to start this conversation digitally or in person, state your observations and intentions, and don't forget those "I" statements. This conversation is about gaining shared understanding, drawing boundaries, and having agreement on how to move forward. This opening statement could sound something like:

"X told me that you made fun of my Y that I told you about. I'm not ok with the fact that you shared with someone else what I told you in confidence, when I told you not to, and you promised me that you wouldn't. It's made me feel like I can't trust you. I don't want to assume the reason you told them – help me understand why you did that."

I know – that's very direct and straight to the point. But it has to be.

Notice that there's *no accusation* in there. You're reporting an observation (what someone reported to you), how it made you feel, drawing the boundary, and seeking to understand that person's why. Yes, it will most likely make that person uncomfortable, but they'll survive. They chose, whether on purpose or not, to share information you told them not to. Being uncomfortable is something they can take responsibility for.

A Scenario with Your Manager

Because this is with your boss, the situation could become a little sticky. If your boss has shared your story with other people when you told them not to, for someone who sits in a position of influence and authority, they have shown bad leadership, a lack of maturity, emotional intelligence and self-awareness. They *should* know better.

You should still seek to understand why they did that, draw the boundary, and make it explicitly clear *again* that they shouldn't do that again. Most importantly, there's a big opportunity here for them to take ownership and role model how to appropriately deal with the situation as your boss.

You could request that your manager approach the person(s) they told about your story and admit their wrongdoing, for example: *"You've already shared the information and made a negative impact. I appreciate that you've said you're sorry, but what would matter more to me is if you tell Y that what you did was wrong and it wasn't your information to share. And, that out of respect to me, you ask them to keep the information to themselves."*

What If They Won't Listen?

If you've addressed the issue with your colleague or boss and they won't take responsibility for what they did or address their disclosure with the people they told, and this has created additional issues for you like bullying from your team or circulating rumors, you may have to consider escalating the situation.

If the issue is about a colleague, consider speaking to your boss and having a three-way mediation session to address the issue.

If the issue is with your boss, you may need to speak to your HR department if you have one, and if you don't, you may need to approach your boss's boss (just breathe). Or, if you feel you need to make a formal complaint, depending on your company's policies, this may result in an HR investigation. No matter the route you choose to take, be clear about what occurred, what your needs are, and what you hope the outcome will be. It's tough, but a necessary boundary to draw for true change.

The outcome of this option is impossible to predict, but what matters is that the behavior from that person ceases, you don't encounter the situation again, and you can hopefully have a *civil* working relationship.

TIP

Please remember this: even if the conversation doesn't go well with someone you've shared with at work, this doesn't mean it won't go well with another person. Give yourself the opportunity to try again with someone else.

I hope this chapter was particularly useful for those of you who have been of two minds of whether or not to share about your mental health at work. I hope it inspired you to reflect on how you feel now and helped you to realize the impact you can have when you do share, as well as giving you some practical steps to take.

We'll now go on to consider this conversation from the other perspective: how to start and have a conversation with a colleague about mental health at work.

TASK
Having a Conversation About Your Mental Health At Work

If you feel ready to speak to someone about your mental health at work (as we discussed on page 105), use what you've learned in this chapter to identify the key points you want to cover so you can do it constructively. Here's a reminder of what to consider:

- *Who* do I want to tell?
- *Why* do I want to tell them?
- *What* do I want to share? If I were to distill my mental health story into "headlines" to be easily shared with this person, what would they say?
- *When* is a good time to share with them?
- Given who this person is, what's the *best way I can explain* things to them so they'll understand?
- What *specific concerns* do I have and how will I explain them?
- What do I want the *desired outcome and next steps* to be?

CHAPTER SUMMARY

- Be honest with yourself about if you're ready to talk about mental health at work. You can choose when you're ready to share – how, with who, and why.
- Personal accountability matters. You have influence in how these conversations go.
- Be constructive in your approach:
  - Choose who you want to talk to, pick the right time and place and make your confidentiality contract.
  - Highlight your goal and your why: speak clearly about what you need, what you want, and how people can support you.
  - Explain if you have concerns.
  - It's ok to get emotional.
  - Aim to educate. Don't assume someone will know exactly what you mean.
  - Address your body language if needed.
  - Consider sharing with your team, manager, or the wider company.

- Don't use mental health as an "excuse" for dropping the ball on something unrelated.
- If someone checks in with you, thank them and let them know it's ok that they asked. If you're not comfortable, set the boundary.
- If the conversation doesn't go well, that's ok. Address it head on and make a plan to move forward. Learn to trust again.

7

HOW TO HAVE CONVERSATIONS ABOUT MENTAL HEALTH AND SUPPORT COLLEAGUES

In this chapter, we'll look in depth at how to support a colleague or team member around mental health at work. This chapter will give you the building blocks for a peer-to-peer conversation.

In the next chapter, we'll look at the *additional* factors to consider as a line manager or team leader when talking to a member of your staff and specific conversational pieces to consider. Everything in this chapter also applies to line managers and leaders, but there are additional elements for them to consider. So, if you're a line manager, senior leader, or company founder, take this chapter to heart as it'll show you the basics and foundations of how to navigate these conversations.

There are five main building blocks for a constructive peer-to-peer mental health conversation:

1. Setting your expectations (before the conversation)
2. How to start the conversation
3. How to listen and what to say
4. What NOT to say: three key things
5. How to respond if your colleagues bring up the conversation

For each of these elements, I'll give you key points to remember and concrete examples of what you can say, based on counselling and coaching techniques.

TIP

A quick note: throughout this chapter I give examples of questions and responses. Use these as a guide, but please make sure that what you say sounds like *you*, in *your* language and style.

SETTING YOUR EXPECTATIONS (BEFORE THE CONVERSATION)

It's wonderful that you want to be a supportive colleague to your work peers. So you can be as constructive and effective as possible, let's take a look at a few elements that will ensure you begin with the right mindset.

YOU CAN MAKE AN IMPACT – BUT YOU'RE NOT A THERAPIST

You don't need to be a trained therapist; you just need to be a supportive empathic human who makes an effort to understand what someone is going through.

Clinical mental health therapists are trained to provide diagnosis and counselling treatment to individuals who have a wide range of mental health conditions. They also provide counselling to people who are going through major life transitions or stress periods that require the support of a clinical professional beyond the capabilities of that person's core *support network*. This is where you come in.

You are *part* of a person's support network. Not *the* support network. That's why it's called a network, not a solo support.

It's not your job to diagnose someone, clinically treat, or counsel them. But, as part of their support network, you play a role in making someone feel heard, seen and supported when they need it. You don't need to be a trained therapist to be empathetic, a good listener, respect someone's privacy, and give them the option of how or if they want help. Anyone can do that, as long as they're willing and know how to do it well. In the coming sections, we'll cover how to do this well from a professional perspective.

You can absolutely be supportive, but remember the role you play in this person's life: to be a supportive co-worker.

TIP

While the techniques in this chapter are based on counselling and coaching, you're *not* having a counselling conversation. You're using some techniques that will be helpful to make your colleague feel heard and understood, in an effective and constructive way.

REMEMBER THE LIMITS OF YOUR ROLE

If a colleague confides in you about what's going on with them, showing vulnerability, you may feel that it's now your sole responsibility to help them (especially for those of you who are natural carers and fixers). This is not true, and a responsibility you shouldn't shoulder alone.

At this stage, you need to remember that you're *not the only* supportive person that your colleague has access to, nor is it solely up to you to be the main driving force that helps your colleague (especially because they ultimately need to help themselves). You may have heard of the "savior complex", where someone is motivated by the need to "save" others in an unhealthy dynamic. Here, your intention needs to be to support *them* – not to fulfill your need to support.

Your job here is to compassionately triage and, based on the situation, to:

- Listen
- Encourage them to take action, self-manage and seek help if needed
- Recommend next steps (if needed or wanted)

It's *not* your responsibility to make your colleague feel better or to solve their issues for them.

It's your role to make them feel heard and supported. A potential *byproduct* of the conversation is that they may feel better after they've discussed their mental health with someone at work who they can trust.

So, your role is clearly defined. To listen, and direct someone to the relevant help if they're ready for it.

In practice, this may be to recommend the conversation be passed on to HR or another appropriate person such as their manager. In this scenario, be explicitly clear that you're *not* trying to avoid the issue, but rather that you're trying to direct them to someone *better suited* to actually give them what they need. What's important here is to explain *why* you're telling them to speak to someone else about this – for their benefit. This could sound something like: *"It sounds like you're completely overloaded. Have you talked to your manager about it? Maybe they could shift some of your projects, or maybe they don't even know you're swamped. Do you feel comfortable to talk to them about it?"*

Additionally, it's useful to be aware of the mental health resources available in your organization, whether it's for yourself or so you can recommend them to others. It could be the employee assistance program, health insurance, wellness app or something else. And, if there aren't resources available in your company, there are private, community, or government resources that are available depending on where you're located. Whether it's a community counselling program or getting counselling through an online pay-as-you-go platform (which are increasing in popularity), being able to recommend something is better than nothing.

CONSIDERATIONS IF YOU WORK IN HR

If you're working in HR, your role will be different if an employee comes to you about needing accommodations for a mental health issue, because that then becomes a larger HR and legal process that your company will (hopefully) have specific policies on how to address. Additionally, how to handle this process from a professional perspective is something that is typically covered off in detail in human resources professional associations in their continuing education modules and at conferences that give the most up-to-date developments in this area. But policy aside, you can still be empathetic, listen, and make this person feel supported. And, if you work in HR and want to share about your own mental health, see page 179.

THERE MAY BE NO CONCLUSION

While it would be great if mental health at work conversations would all go swimmingly smooth, with the person feeling great at the end and there being a clear plan to move forward, that isn't the reality we live in. Mental health is complex, and so are the conversations, and that's ok.

Make sure to set your expectations that you want to be supportive to your colleague, but that it's not about going from A to B in one conversation.

DON'T ASSUME IT'S MENTAL ILLNESS

Before you label your colleague with a mental illness because of how they may be acting, bear in mind that they could just be going through a rough time.

As we discussed in Chapter 1, stress and mental illness can present similarly, but stress itself is not a diagnosable mental illness. If you're observing that a colleague's behavior is "peculiar" or has changed, don't make assumptions about why – and don't try to diagnose them!

Observe, observe, observe.

Think about that person's baseline behavior as you know it to be, and consider:

- Have the behaviors they've displayed or the things they've said changed recently?
- Are you noticing a pattern?

When you do have that conversation, whether they bring it up or you do, seek to understand what's causing the behavior change – don't assume or suggest its origin.

HOW TO START THE CONVERSATION

Beginning the conversation can often feel like the toughest part. Here we'll cover some essential points to consider as you begin a conversation to check-in on someone's emotional health.

CREATE SPACE, BUT ACCEPT IT MAY NOT BE THE RIGHT TIME

If you approach your colleague to chat, ask them if it's a good time for it. If they say they want to, but can't at that moment because they're busy or not in the right headspace, then ask when would suit them, and arrange an alternative time. Take their scheduling lead so they don't feel pressured.

If they say they don't want to chat, you *need* to be ok with them saying no, or not now. State that they have the option, without the obligation. If your offer is turned down for whatever reason, you could simply respond with: *"No pressure at all, I just wanted to check in. I hope that's ok. I'm here if and when you want to talk."*

If you approach your colleague about their mental health, and they say they're fine and that they've just had a bad headache (or some other form of physical illness that's deemed more "socially acceptable" than experiencing negative emotions), that may be a signal that they aren't ready to talk or that they're embarrassed to open up. If that happens, gently ask again later, to give them another opportunity to tell you what's really going on. Don't make them feel like they've been caught in a lie, but rather that you're concerned and want to let them know it's ok to open up about what's actually going on. A gentle nudge could sound like: *"Sorry to hear you have a headache. I hope you don't mind my asking, but is that really what's bothering you? You've not seemed yourself lately, and I just wanted to check in on you."*

If at that stage they insist it's a physical ailment, take the hint and don't push any more. Again, let them know that you're around to chat if and when they want to.

CONSIDER THE TIME, PLACE AND MEDIUM

In the last chapter we discussed the considerations around picking the right time, place, and medium to share about *your* mental health at work (page 111). The same guidance goes for reaching out to a colleague about *theirs*. A few reminders:

- Don't try to start a conversation when you know the person has an impending deadline, during a work call, or another time that seems like it may not land well. Use your gut and exercise judgment. Ask yourself, *"If someone was going to talk to me about my emotional health, when would be a reasonable time for them to bring it up?"*
- Choose the medium that you feel would be useful to reach out on. Can the two of you speak in person? On a call or on video? If you're going to speak via tech, aim for video if possible so you can see the person's body language (as we discussed on page 112).
- Consider the medium where that person is most comfortable. Do they tend to divulge more on chat? Do they prefer video? Try to take this into account as you make the decision on the medium choice.

START WITH A QUESTION AND OBSERVATION

Try to begin with a simple open-ended question – a question designed to provoke a fuller answer with additional detail rather than just a "yes" or "no". Don't make it complicated. A complicated question may receive a complicated answer. A simple open-ended question might be: *"What's been going on?"* Follow this with an observation to explain why you're asking.

You won't *always* be able to use an open-ended question to start off a mental health conversation. You may need to use a closed question (with a yes or no answer, e.g. *"Are you alright?"*) that's coupled with an observation.

TIP

Consider your tone (calm and genuine is ideal) and be deliberate with your word usage.

Share Your Observation

Here, it's good to use the noticing technique – a consistently used method in both counselling and coaching. It shows you how to signal to someone that you're sharing an observation from patterns you've seen over time, and that you're calling attention to a specific set of behaviors. To do this, use "I" statements and also use the word "seem" in your sentence. This way you're making it clear this is your observation – your *perception* of the situation. And, you're not implying that this is a fact for what they've been feeling or behaving. "Seem" gives them the chance to explain and clarify and doesn't dictate how you think they feel.

Include Your "Why"

You don't want it to seem like you've been "watching them". Creepy and not ideal. *"I've been watching you closely for weeks, and you seem off. Tell me, what's going on?!"* That's obviously an example of what *not* to do! Don't make your colleague feel like you've been operating the microscope or give them cause to fear you.

Rather, you want to show that you've been noticing how they're doing, as a human and as a colleague; that you're paying attention because you *care*. That's your why.

Sharing an observation about someone's behavior without explaining what you're trying to accomplish by sharing it with them is a recipe for making someone feel defensive.

The Ideal Start

The best starter to a conversation uses observations and caring-focused wording that invites a conversation, from a casual place, as opposed to make someone feel under investigation.

As an equation, it would look like this:

Genuine tone + deliberate word choice

+

"I" statement of noticing and observation with use of "seem"

+

Open-ended question format

+

Your "why" of compassion and concern

=

A caring and gentle start

A few opening examples:

- *"I've noticed you've seemed a bit down the last few weeks. Just wanted to make sure you're ok. What's been going on?"*
- *"I noticed that you teared up a little at the end of our last team Zoom call – are you alright? Did you want to have a catch-up?"*
- *"I don't want to assume, but you seem like you've been going through a rough patch at the moment – is everything ok?"*

Now that we've looked at the opening questions to start the conversation, let's consider how to keep the conversation going, how to listen, and what to say.

HOW TO LISTEN AND WHAT TO SAY

Once your colleague has said they want to talk, this is where the *actual support* happens. The points here can feel like a lot to take in. In reality, this section all boils down to choosing your words wisely and listening well. It breaks down into:

- Looking for the breadcrumbs
- Using little lead-ins
- Asking the right question early on
- Following their vibe and lead
- Actively listening, without judgment
- Reflecting and clarifying
- Normalizing
- Seeking to understand their individual situation
- Offering encouragement, empathy, and a supportive response
- Offering stories (if desired)
- Offering an alternative perspective (if desired)
- Asking action-oriented questions

LOOK FOR THE BREADCRUMBS

Just because someone wants to talk to you doesn't mean they'll have their thoughts organized and ready to go, especially if this is the first time they've gotten support from a colleague. Nerves may be running high and they may have trouble stringing their thoughts together – and that's ok.

Look for the breadcrumbs which may be a signal that they want to say more. *"I'm hanging in, doing so-so"* may be a signal for, *"I don't feel good, but I don't want to burden you."* Or they may say something more explicit, but stop just shy of getting over the line like, *"It's been a hell of a month, I'm not sure anyone would get it."* But they really want to say, *"I want to talk about this, but I'm worried you or others may not understand me."*

USE LITTLE LEAD-INS

If you notice these breadcrumbs, use open-ended questions and acknowledge what they've said. Provide them with the "permission" that it's ok to proceed forward with you and create the space for the person to come out from behind the wall. You can do this by using little lead-in questions and statements to get them started.

If you encounter a breadcrumb trail statement, helpful lead-in questions would sound something like:

- *"Hanging in? Sounds a little stressful – what's going on?"*
- *"I might understand, how about giving it a go and explaining it to me?"*

ASK THE RIGHT QUESTION EARLY ON

In the last chapter we talked about the importance of stating what you need from someone when talking about your mental health (Highlight Your Goal and Your Why, page 113). The inverse applies here: ask the person what *they want* out of the conversation and what would be the most useful for them.

Ask the question explicitly and let them inform you. Do they want you to listen while they vent? Do they want your guidance? This could sound like: *"I'm happy you want to talk. Do you want me to just listen or do you want help sorting through things?"*

Keep in mind that not everyone will know what they need in the start of the conversation, and that's ok. If they say they don't know, encourage them to start talking with an open-ended statement (a statement that provokes an answer beyond a yes or no). Examples of open-ended statements are:

- *"Ok, tell me what's going on."*
- *"Help me understand how you're feeling."*
- *"Help me understand the context of what's been happening this month."*

Once you ask the question, be patient and listen.

FOLLOW THE VIBE AND THEIR LEAD

If your colleague needs to cry or get angry, let them.

Those are healthy emotions and catharsis (the process of releasing emotions and feeling relief from that process) is healthy. The instinct to comfort and dampen down negative emotions, or even go into toxic positivity mode, may unintentionally kick in and you may say something like, *"It's ok, don't cry."* What's actually *more* helpful is, *"It's ok to be upset. What's going on?"*

If they use humor as a way of processing how they're feeling, or poking at themselves, and they want you to be a bit jovial to lighten the mood to make it more comfortable, follow their lead. Most people will set the tone and pace if you listen, observe, and follow.

ACTIVELY LISTEN, WITHOUT JUDGMENT

There are two important points to listening effectively: listen actively and without judgment.

Active Listening

This is a crucial skill that *many* people struggle with. Whether it's being constantly distracted by technology, being focused on something else, or just being impatient – it's a skill that everyone could brush up on.

Simply put, active listening is when you're *really* engaging with what someone is saying and how they're saying it. You're present in that moment with them, and you hear what they're saying without judgment or dispensing advice. (We'll shortly go over *why* you shouldn't be giving advice in these sorts of conversations, unless explicitly asked for by the other person, and that's even as a last resort.)

Make your colleague feel as though you're *really* listening to them and not thinking of other things. Simple ways to do this are through nodding your head, making acknowledgment sounds (e.g. "mmhmm"), and asking the right questions and giving helpful responses to further the conversation (more on this below). Try to do this naturally so it doesn't seem staged.

Explicit Non-judgment

Many people (more than you might think) are really comforted by hearing someone explicitly say to them that they aren't being judged for something they share. Be explicit that you won't judge or view them differently for their disclosure around their mental health. While you would hope and assume they'd know this by them choosing to speak with you, they may not.

One of the personal roadblocks in Chapter 4 on page 76 was that people don't speak up about their mental health because of guilt or shame they feel based on conditioning, or bad past experiences, they may have had throughout their life. Here, you want to immediately put that to rest. It can even be a good way to get the conversation going, in case your colleague is a bit nervous. You could try:

- *"It's nothing to be ashamed of. Talking about this won't change how I look at you."*
- *"You can share whatever you need to – there won't be any judgment from me."*

REFLECT AND CLARIFY

Reflective and clarifying techniques are very well used in the person-centered and humanistic approach to counselling, popularized by psychologist Carl Rogers (as mentioned on page 76), and many other person-centered-focused psychologists.

Harvard Health Publishing noted that the person-centered approach is built on the idea of asking the right non-directive questions to help someone tell their own story so they can decide how they would like to proceed, as opposed to directing them down a certain path of thinking.[58] This approach is still widely used in counselling and in coaching by those that subscribe to this method of support and facilitating change. Let's have a look at these two techniques.

Reflecting is where you verbalize and show that you've heard what the person has said. Examples of this might sound like:

- Statement: *"So what I'm hearing you say is..."* or *"It sounds like you're describing..."*
- Question: *"It sounds like you're describing X, Y, Z – am I understanding correctly?"*

Clarifying is used to explain that you're not quite sure what they're saying, with the aim that you'd like to understand better. Examples of this might sound like:

- Statement: *"I'm not quite sure I follow what you're saying. I want to understand – explain it to me one more time please."*
- Question: *"I don't think I'm getting exactly what you mean. Can you please explain it a different way?"*

Resist the urge to feel like you're probing – you're not. By reflecting back what you've heard, or by asking for clarification, it shows that you're actively listening and care about what your colleague is saying. And who knows, they may not have had someone truly listen to them in a long time.

NORMALIZE

Normalization is one of the most *important* techniques to use. It's a technique I've used constantly with both clinical and coaching clients over the years, and in my group facilitation and event seminars. Normalizing is simply reminding the person that they are not alone in how they feel. That many others have gone through similar struggles.

Here's what this could look like in practice. Let's say that your colleague has shared with you that they struggle with a mental health condition or they're so stressed that they're edging toward burning out. Your normalizing response would sound something like:

- *"Feeling that way is really common – there are so many people who struggle with this. I promise you're not alone."*
- *"There's no need to feel ashamed about feeling this, we all feel that emotion for a reason, to let us know something is up."*

SEEK TO UNDERSTAND THEIR INDIVIDUAL EXPERIENCE

Normalizing is important, but remember that just because many other people may struggle with something similar doesn't mean you know *exactly* how they feel.

If someone is struggling with their mental health, a mental illness, or something going on in their lives that's impacting them at work, a typical well-intended response might be, *"I know someone else who dealt with this, and if they can overcome it, you can too!"* No, don't say that.

While this is benevolently intended to give the person hope, the result is that they may feel that you're just comparing them to someone else and not listening to how they feel. Your colleague is an individual and should be treated as such. Try asking: *"So I can understand better, what's it been like specifically for you?"*

Normalizing is not telling people to "deal with it like this other person did"; it's letting the person know they aren't alone.

RESPECT PRIVACY AND CONFIDENTIALITY

Make sure that your colleague knows you won't talk to others about what they tell you. Make sure they know they can trust you. Acknowledge the confidentiality of the conversation. This could be through simple statements like:

- *"No worries at all, all of this will stay with me."*
- *"I wouldn't disrespect you by sharing this with others – you have my word."*

SUICIDAL CONCERNS

An important exception to confidentiality is if someone discloses to you that they have suicidal feelings. Suicide is an *incredibly* common issue around the world. I've lost count of the number of clinical clients I had who were suicidal. I've seen many employee lives lost to suicide at several companies.

If a colleague discloses to you that they're having suicidal feelings, their safety becomes the number one priority. And, in that moment, you're *not* the best person to help them. The best thing you can do is to get them access to someone trained to deal with the situation.

There are two types of suicidal thoughts: passive and active. Passive suicidal thoughts sound something like, *"I'm tired of feeling depressed, I don't want to be here, and I don't think anyone would miss me."* Whereas active suicidal thoughts are when someone has access to a dangerous method that could end their life, and plans to use it. This would sound something like, *"I can't take this anymore, I have several bottles of pills at home that I'm considering taking."* Bear in mind all you know is what they tell you: you can't know the full extent of their thoughts. Therefore, any mention of suicidal thoughts requires immediate attention.

What You Should Do

The best way you can help that person is by connecting them to emergency-trained professionals, clinical staff, or potentially HR if they have emergency protocols to connect those people to resources. Clearly explain to your colleague that you're concerned about their safety and it's important to get them access to professional help straight away.

This is not a betrayal of their trust – it's prioritizing their safety. Yes, it's true, they may not be thrilled with you for doing this, but their safety is more important than what they think of you at that moment.

A helpful way to phrase this is: *"You've just said you feel suicidal and I'm worried about you. I respect your privacy, truly, but you've mentioned hurting yourself and what's really important right now is getting you access to help, and quickly. I really think we need to speak with X. How about we do that together?"*

Typically speaking, and especially when you offer to support this person to reach out for emergency help, people will *generally* accept the offer – especially when they see the care someone is showing them.

If they decline your offer, while it may be uncomfortable, you may need to tell them that you don't feel comfortable leaving that conversation unattended and that, from an ethical and safety standpoint, you need to inform the appropriate person (e.g. calling the EAP, a suicide hotline, HR or a health and safety person at your company – depending on your company's setup and resources).

OFFER ENCOURAGEMENT, EMPATHY AND A SUPPORTIVE RESPONSE

Encouragement, empathy and being supportive are the best ways to keep the conversation rolling along. They're kind of like the guard rails along a bowling alley, so the ball doesn't fall into the gutter.

Encouragement

To be encouraging is to prompt someone gently, to show that you want to know more, and that it's ok for them to continue sharing. Here are some simple phrases to use:

- *"Tell me more about that piece."*
- *"I hear what you're saying."*
- *"No, you're fine, please keep going."* (This one is useful if your colleague starts back pedaling and saying things like *"I need to stop complaining, I'm sorry".*)

Empathy

Show empathy by making an effort to truly understand the feelings of that person. And even though you can't understand *exactly* how they feel, you can acknowledge what they've told you in a caring way. You can let them know that in the conversation it's ok to come as they are and that they don't need to hide their negative emotions or anything that may feel "heavy". Some empathic statements are:

- *"I can see why you'd feel that way after that happened."*
- *"That sounds like a lot – I'd feel really stressed out too!"*
- *"It's totally reasonable that you feel that way – I can see how you got from A to B."*

Being Supportive

Being supportive is really about letting your colleague know you're there for them and that you appreciated that they've opened up to *you*. Remember your role as a supportive colleague that we discussed on page 138, and frame it in that context. Some supportive statements are:

- *"We work together closely, I'm happy to be there for you and I'm confident you'd do it for me if I needed it."*
- *"I appreciate you trusting me enough to talk about this."*
- *"I don't mind having catch-ups from time to time, truly."*

While these statements may seem rudimentary, they pack a punch. It helps your colleague know that you don't mind, and are happy to support them in this conversation.

OFFER STORIES (IF DESIRED)

If someone is feeling alone in their struggle, you may feel it's appropriate to offer up related stories if you have them. Sometimes hearing stories about other people who have dealt with a similar thing can be comforting to hear. If the story is about you (and they want to hear it), it can help to build rapport and connectedness in your conversation.

However, let your colleague *choose* whether or not they want to hear these stories. You want to give the option without the obligation, so your colleague can decide if it would be helpful for them. If you start recanting stories without asking permission, this *reeks* of not truly listening.

Here's how posing that question could sound:

"I have a very close friend who went through something similar based on what you're describing. Would it be helpful if I told you about it and what helped them? You can say no if you want, I just wanted to offer"

OFFER AN ALTERNATIVE PERSPECTIVE (IF DESIRED)

Do not offer an alternative perspective at the beginning of a conversation. At the start of a conversation about mental health or mental illness, even if you have pre-existing rapport with your colleague, you haven't built enough rapport around the topic or learned enough detail from your colleague to offer an alternative perspective.

If your colleague seems to be looking at a situation with their mental health in a way that may be counterproductive or unhelpful, or their words are in conflict with how they said they've dealt with things (this is called dissonance), it could be an opportunity to *gently* challenge how they're looking at the situation.

This is the type of moment to *offer* an alternative perspective or way of thinking, but you *must* ask if they want this. If you offer it without their consent, you may appear as though you're trying to *fix* when it hasn't been asked for.

Your colleague will appreciate that you offered them the option as opposed to diving right in. You could ask:

- *"Would it be useful if I suggest a different way to think about this? No obligation, just an offer."*
- *"Is it helpful if I mention a different way to go about dealing with this? Totally up to you."*

Reframing

When it comes to offering an alternative way to look at something your colleague has disclosed, or bringing up a perspective they may not have considered, you'll be introducing new data into their "system" – information that they may not have thought of, yet.

This idea of gently suggesting other thought patterns or beliefs to challenge feelings or look at a situation differently is rooted in Cognitive-Behavioral Therapy (CBT), and is called reframing. The alternative thought patterns help the person look at an issue in a more constructive way (as opposed to an unhelpful way) and gain insight to encourage change and growth. If your colleague has welcomed alternative perspectives or thoughts, you could try:

- *"Based on what you've said, and I hope you don't mind my asking, but have you thought about looking at it X way?"*
- *"Are there things in your control that you could shift to help with this?"*
- *"You said that X is really hard for you, but that you're not sure how else to think about it. Have you thought about Y?"*

ASK ACTION-ORIENTED QUESTIONS

If your colleague invites your help on where to take the conversation next, then you need to ask action-oriented questions so that the decision *comes from them*. If they've invited it, you can include some suggestions embedded within your questions, but your questions need to be centered on their *readiness* and what they're willing to do. These questions could sound like:

- *"What do you want to try that might help with this?*
- *"It sounds like you might want to talk to your manager about this. Do you feel ready for that?"*
- *"It sounds like you might want to talk to a counselor. I know a lot of people who have found that to be helpful. Have you talked to HR about our insurance options?"*

MAKE SURE YOU'RE BOTH CLEAR ON ANY NEXT STEPS

Be clear on how you're closing out the conversation, so it's not left on an uncertain note.

Is there an employee assistance program or HR department in your company that you will refer the person to? Do they want you to just check in with them in a few weeks? Is there no need for follow-up and they just wanted to vent? To achieve this, and make sure you're both aligned, you need to – you guessed it – ask the right questions.

A good counselling and coaching tactic to use here is something called summarizing – summing up what you've heard from the person and then tying that to the agreed-upon action. Additionally, if it's appropriate in the moment, include a timeframe so it makes them feel accountable to themselves to take action on next steps. So, these summarizing statements could sound like:

- *"I'm happy we got a chance to talk. It sounds like you want to talk to X later this week. Feel free to let me know how it goes."*
- *"Thanks for coming to me about this. Let's have another virtual coffee in two weeks, how does that sound?"*
- *"Sounds like you're doing alright now – and I really hope you feel better soon."*

WHAT NOT TO SAY

DON'T FILL SILENCE, JUST SIT WITH IT

If you reach a point in the conversation where you don't know what to say, that's ok.

Silence can be uncomfortable for people because it can feel awkward, but silence is quite useful, particularly for the person who is sharing. They may need time to gather their thoughts or name what it is they're feeling. This is also a key skill used in counselling and coaching, allowing the "space" to do its work.

If your colleague doesn't know what to say, that's alright too. After a few moments of silence, it can be helpful to say something like: *"It's ok not to know where to start, just start talking and we'll see where it goes. Take the time you need and let me know how I can be helpful."*

AVOID SUPERLATIVE OR EXAGGERATED LANGUAGE

I can't stress this enough: *be intentional* with your language choice.

As we talked about in Chapter 3 (page 40), the language we use matters. And if your colleague has opened up to you about their mental health, this is *the* most important time to be intentional with the words you choose. Most people will take you for what you mean based on exactly what comes out of your mouth and how it lands with them.

Keep in mind that using inaccurate language to describe what someone is feeling can be triggering for people and may make them feel unintentionally attacked. In my clinical work, and also organizational work, I've found that people *really* don't like to be misunderstood when it comes to their thoughts, emotions, feelings and behaviors. They feel as though they've been mislabeled. Feeling understood is, after all, a core human need. And, when it comes to mental health conversations, that matters a lot.

There's a big difference between: *"That does sound hard, I can see talking about this seems a painful for you,"* and *"WHOA, that's insane. Sounds like you went crazy. I can feel the flames radiating off of you right now."*

If you're prone to say whatever comes into your head without thinking, pause. Create space between what they've said and your response. Try using reflecting and clarifying statements and questions (see page 150). By repeating back your colleague's words, you can literally say what they've said, so it's representative of how they've described feeling.

DON'T GIVE ADVICE – SEEK TO UNDERSTAND

When I was in clinical practice, I remember the urge to give advice. I still get that urge now when I do coaching for leaders. Sometimes, my clients just plainly ask me for advice. In those moments, even when asked, giving advice is not helpful, because it prevents people from considering the options for themselves, what's specifically *right for them,* and is not usually what people need. There are occasions where it can be appropriate, *but* that's after they've explored all of their other self-guided reflection options.

TIP

By seeking to understand, and asking the right questions, you will help your colleague feel heard. Encourage them to explore options if they're ready to based on *their own* experience and needs – not based on your advice to them.

Also, while your advice may be well intended, it may unintentionally feel like an affront, as if you're not listening. Instead, you're automatically comparing yourself to them, when this should be about *them*, not you.

A misstep in this area could sound something like, *"I've noticed that you've seemed blue in recent weeks. Why don't you work out? That always helps me when I feel low energy."* This may result in the receiving person's potential internal thought to be: *"Hmm, nice that he checked in, but he has no idea that I have clinical depression and that isn't the same... why is he giving me advice?"* and potential external response of: *"I'm doing ok, thanks for asking though."*

Right there, an opportunity to connect has been lost.

By seeking to understand what's going on, you're showing higher emotional intelligence. Bill Murphy Jr., a contributing writer to Inc.com, framed this well when discussing emotional intelligence in conversations, particularly about an archetype called The Advice Giver.[59] Murphy explained how The Advice Giver tends to give advice because it comes naturally to them, and because it's easy, using their own problems or experiences as a reference point (which is the opposite of what we want to do here). The biggest obstacle here is that The Advice Giver (or anyone who jumps into giving advice) doesn't focus on *asking questions* – one of the most important parts of supporting someone. Murphy explained, and I agree, that a supportive response (as discussed earlier) is what keeps the conversation focused on the other person and what is, ultimately, most helpful.

In some cases, the person you're speaking with may *really* want advice because they feel uncertain and confused about how to handle their mental health struggle that may be impacting them at work. In *some cases* (and this is if they really push you), make sure you've first gone through how they feel about it and the options they've explored. Tell them that while you can suggest some options to them, that *they* ultimately need to pick what works for them.

BE MINDFUL OF YOUR BODY LANGUAGE AND EYE CONTACT

Eye Contact

Maintaining eye contact can be uncomfortable for some people, and that's not even taking into account potential cultural practices (e.g. in some cultures, making direct eye contact can be seen as aggressive or disrespectful, especially toward older people). Try to make this natural and find a balance – not avoiding eye contact, but also not staring. In the absence of visuals (e.g. if you're on the phone) you'll need to be more aware of your vocal tones.

Body Language

If you're chatting in person or on video, try to be open with your body language. If you sit with your arms crossed or leaning away from them, the receiver could experience you as distant, even if it's just how you sit comfortably. Show that you're present and not squirming. A helpful tip here from my counselling days is to do something called mirroring (mimicking their body language in a similar way). Don't be painfully obvious about it, but you get the idea.

Observe *their* body language (if they seem uncomfortable or at ease). Remember, nonverbal cues are important in knowing how someone is feeling. These observations can be useful in helping someone to feel at ease if they appear not to be. It can be as simple as stating the observation and asking, *"You look a little uncomfortable. I don't want to assume why – is it something I've said or is it what we're discussing?"*

IF YOUR COLLEAGUE BRINGS UP THE CONVERSATION

If a colleague approaches you at work, either in person or digitally, to check-in about their emotional health, that is a *big* compliment. If your colleague feels psychologically safe enough to talk to you about a delicate and personal topic, clearly, you've been doing something right.

Everything discussed in this chapter so far all still applies. However, there are a few additional pointers to consider to make sure you react in the most helpful way.

COMMEND THEIR COURAGE

Tell them that you really appreciate that they felt comfortable enough to speak with you and remind them of the bravery it took to speak up.

As we discussed earlier, people can feel wrongful guilt, shame or weakness in general when speaking up about mental health or a mental health condition. Let them know that speaking up took strength and self-awareness. Be authentic and casual in how you say this, otherwise it may come off as though you're kid-gloving them and trying to give a proverbial gold star, which may seem condescending. Saying this well could sound like: *"I know you said you were nervous to tell me, but I appreciate that you did. That couldn't have been easy."*

TAKE THE TIME AND PLACE INTO ACCOUNT

Similar to when you are considering the right time and place for your colleague, you also need to consider your availability this time, too.

If your colleague has come to you wanting to discuss their mental health, and they did it at a time where you have a deadline and can't give them the attention they need, make sure you explain about this and that carving out a time to chat is important to you. This will let them know that you've acknowledged their request and are ensuring that you can both talk about it at a time where you can be present to hear them. This could sound like*: "I have a deadline in an hour, but I really want to talk about this with you and give you my full attention. Can we chat at 5pm?"*

MINIMIZE DISTRACTIONS

Imagine if you were trying to talk to someone about something really important to you, potentially for the first time, and they were distracted by tech. You'd assume that what was coming through on one of their screens was more important than what you had to say, and you were potentially nervous to say. It may make you feel ignored – which doesn't feel good. Give the conversation your full attention and the respect it deserves. Short of the world burning or someone dying, everything else can wait.

Put your phone face down. Close the laptop. (Unless you're speaking with them on the phone or on the computer.)

We've covered a lot of material in this chapter and looked at how to support a colleague about their mental health at work in depth. In the next chapter, we'll move on to consider some specific considerations as a manager or leader when discussing mental health with your team members.

TASK
Try To Have A Conversation

Think of a colleague that you've been concerned about or "meaning to talk to".

Review the points in this chapter on how to approach the conversation and, ahead of time, write down the basics of what you're going to say. Use the examples as a starter, but edit these so they sound like your voice.

Consider:

- Your opening question, observation and include your "why" (page 145)
- Drafting a few:
  - Lead-in statements (page 147)
  - Reflective and clarifying questions (page 150)
  - Normalizing statements (page 151)
  - Statements of empathy and encouragement (page 154)
- What your action-oriented question might be (page 158)

Brush up on your company's available mental health resources so you can draw upon these if needed. If there aren't any, consider googling relevant resources (e.g. online counselling platforms) so you can have it ready in case it comes up in conversation.

You now have the building blocks you need for a conversation. Now... it's time to have a go.

A few final tips before you go for it:

- I don't recommend having this script right in front of you when you chat with the person (!) but do review it ahead of time. It will make you feel more confident in the moment.

- Don't put pressure on yourself to nail all points mentioned. That's a tall order. If you can cover a good portion of them, you'll have done a good job.
- Start small with one conversation. Be mindful about who you'd like to start it with (don't just pick someone random).
- Remember, if this is a new skill for you, be kind to yourself.

CHAPTER SUMMARY

- Set your expectations before the conversation: you can have an impact, you're not their therapist, and don't assume your colleague has a mental illness.
- Start the conversation by creating space, being mindful of time and place, being ok with no, state your why, and start with simple questions.
- Actively listen, follow the breadcrumbs, ask what kind of support they want, follow their lead, don't judge, ask reflective and clarifying questions, normalize, offer empathy, encouragement, and support, and offer alternative thoughts or stories of others only if your colleague says it will be helpful.
- Don't fill the silence with unhelpful words, don't use exaggerated language, and don't give advice. Seek to understand.
- Understand what to do if your colleague shares suicidal thoughts – engage resources immediately.
- If your colleagues bring up the conversation: everything applies as if you were bringing it up, but also commend them for their courage, take your availability into account so you can be present for them, and minimize distractions.

8

LEADERS AND MANAGERS

How to Set the Tone and Discuss Mental Health with Your Team Members

Good news: the conversational building blocks of Chapter 7 apply to you if you are a manager, team leader, senior leader in the business – or some other synonym of that. However, in your leadership position, there are some additional factors you'll need to take into account.

No matter how "flat" your organization may be, if you manage a team, you sit in a position of authority. With this authority comes the real, and perceived, power dynamics that accompany your role.

Some managers think that having constructive and compassionate conversations about mental health with their team members is outside of their remit or that they can't make an impact. This simply isn't true.

You can make an impact – in fact, quite a big one. A team member that knows their manager actually cares about their mental health will be a key contributor to building that psychological safe work environment we discussed in Chapter 5 (page 86), where they can do their best work. For some, the existence of, or lack of care around this topic at work, can make or break someone's employee experience.

My interviewee L shows an example of how to "do it right" as a manager, giving to her team what she would hope to get from her own leader. Below, she describes her approach on how to be a line manager that enables mental health conversations and sets the tone *clearly* in the team:

"When I was a line manager, I didn't see my team members as assets, resource, or human capital (the worst phrase ever) that can be used or discarded. I saw them as human beings, and as such, we're going to get to know each other, and build trust. I was open with people about my own challenges and invited them to share stuff with me. Anytime they felt they were not getting the support they needed, whether it's in their role or on a personal level, I wanted to know about it, because then, I could support them. If I don't know, I can't support them. I have been the person on the other side of the conversation who had a manager who was clueless, who didn't invite me to speak up or bring my whole self to work, and it was the worst thing. I never want there to be any shame for having a mental health challenge." L, a Black female working in the consulting industry

R had some really good guidance on providing the same flexibility for mental health and mental illness as a leader (hopefully) would for physical health:

"Some people will need time off, some people will need just a talk, some will need other support, and it's very individual. But it's no different in many ways from a physical health condition. If someone gets a hip replacement, they are going to be off for a period of time and they're going to need to recuperate, and when they come back to the office you might need to provide them with additional support that they might need to work slightly differently for a while. Why should it be different with mental illness?" R, a Caucasian male lawyer

With this in mind, before we take a look at how to set you up for successful discussions with your team members about mental health at work, we first need to take a look at *you*.

CHECK IN WITH YOURSELF FIRST

Before you can start creating a culture where discussions around mental health are normalized in your team, it's important to first look at how *you* feel about having these sorts of conversations with your team members.

In order to do this, you'll need to consider and reflect on your own roadblocks, like the outside- and inside-of-work factors we discussed in Chapters 4 and 5. Regardless of where you sit in the business, you're an individual and you bring your beliefs and experiences about mental health and mental illness into work. Based on your experiences and potential roadblocks, you may need to tinker with some of your views around talking about your own mental health before you're able to address your team. How can you be expected to have open conversations about mental health or mental illness as a leader with your team, if you as an individual have uncertainties or discomfort around those topics you haven't addressed yet?

TIP

It's up to you to decide the impact you want to make – not only as an individual, but as a leader with influence.

If you're nervous or uncomfortable about talking about mental health, that's normal and absolutely ok. Talking about mental health at work, especially when in a leadership position, takes courage and vulnerability.

Here are some of the common fears I hear from leaders around talking about this topic at work, particularly with their team members:

- *"I don't want to say the wrong thing and make them feel awkward or worse."*
- *"I'm their boss. Mental health is personal, I don't think I'm allowed to bring that up to them."* (FYI this is compartmentalization.)
- *"I'm not a therapist. What if I 'open Pandora's box' and they start coming to me all the time?"*

Have you ever thought something similar to one of the above statements? It's ok if you did. You're not alone. It's like learning a new language. How are you supposed to be automatically fluent at it?

You need to check in with yourself about what your fears are around discussing this topic. Whether it's a fear in discussing it with your team, or even speaking up about your own challenges, having clarity is helpful.

BE REALLY HONEST WITH YOURSELF

The questions below will help you unpack your thoughts around mental health at work. Before we look at working through your thoughts and feelings, there's one crucial thing to be aware of: you need to be *very* honest with yourself when answering these questions.

If you determine from your answers that the hesitation to discuss this topic is from "your own stuff" (outside of work beliefs and experiences), you'll hopefully become more aware of these personal roadblocks, and make a plan to shift how you'd like to constructively approach this topic at work as a leader, and with your team.

If you determine that your hesitation to discuss this topic is based on a wider precedent that's set in the company you work for (roadblocks from within the business), then there may be an opportunity for you as a leader to start the conversation and shift the narrative (similar to Sharing Your Story Company-wide on page 119). You could put feelers out to see if there is a willingness or desire from other leaders in the business to join you in this effort. Easier said than done, but something important to consider. *Many* of the businesses I've spoken to and consulted for hadn't spoken about mental health *at all* yet, let alone mental illness, and the people who got me in the door to change that... were leaders.

There are five questions to ask yourself in order to get a clear picture of your feelings toward mental health at work, as a manager. Ask yourself:

1. DO YOU HAVE PERSONAL CONCERNS ABOUT HOW THESE CONVERSATIONS WILL GO?

Ask yourself:

- What are your specific concerns or hesitations? What do you think will happen if these conversations "don't go well"?
- Are your concerns based on your personal experiences or opinions about mental health or mental illness outside of work? What happened that made you feel this way?
- Are these concerns based in fear of the unknown?

Commitment to action: After reflecting on these concerns, are you willing to move on from them so you can approach these conversations willingly and with open mindedness?

TIP

Revisit Chapters 1, 2, 5 and 6 (and the tasks within them) to help you answer these.

---

2. DO YOU FEEL EQUIPPED AS A MANAGER TO HAVE THESE CONVERSATIONS WITH YOUR TEAM?

Ask yourself:

- If yes, why? If no, why not?
- What would being "equipped" for these conversations look like skill-wise?
- Do you know anyone in the business that seems to handle these conversations well with their team? What have you observed that made you think that?
- If you don't feel equipped, what resources can you use to learn about this topic both in and outside of work?
- Who can you speak to in the business that knows about this topic?

Commitment to action: What specific one or two actions do you want to focus on to equip yourself for these conversations? Learning from a leadership peer? Define what "success" looks like for you here.

TIP

This chapter will equip you with specific guidance on what to say and how to approach this as a manager/leader.

---

3. DO YOU, AS A LEADER IN THE BUSINESS, FEEL COMFORTABLE SPEAKING UP ABOUT YOUR OWN MENTAL HEALTH?

Ask yourself:

- If yes, why? If no, why not?
- How does this influence your willingness to disclose information about your mental health to your team members?

- Have you observed or heard about other leaders in the business sharing about their mental health?
- Have you observed interactions or behaviors at your company that have made you feel uncomfortable speaking up as a leader?
- Is it important to you that you make an impact as a leader in the business about normalizing mental health discussions at work? If so, why?

Commitment to action: Are you willing to speak up about your own mental health, at least to your team? When will you do this?

TIP

Chapters 3 and 5 are particularly helpful in answering these questions.

---

4. DO YOU FEEL THAT YOU HAVE PERMISSION TO TALK TO YOUR OWN MANAGER ABOUT YOUR MENTAL HEALTH?

Ask yourself:

- If yes, why? If no, why not?
- Are your feelings based on your assumptions or actual interactions you've had with your manager?

Commitment to action: If you haven't yet, when will you talk to your manager about this? How do you want to approach it?

TIP

Chapters 3, 4, 5, and 6 are helpful here in answering these questions.

---

5. WHAT ARE YOUR SPECIFIC GOALS OF DISCUSSING MENTAL HEALTH AT WORK WITH YOUR TEAM MEMBERS?

Ask yourself:

- Is this a tick-box exercise for you?
- Do you want them to feel safer to speak up so you can be a tight-knit team?
- Do you want to share more about yourself to improve your rapport with them?
- How would you approach this process effectively and authentically?
- How do you want them to experience your leadership around mental health (e.g. your role modeling)?

Commitment to action: Decide your main goal(s) in discussing mental health with your team.

TIP

This chapter will help you with these areas. Also revisit Highlight Your Goal and Your Why in Chapter 6 (page 113).

TASK
Reflect On Your Mindset Shift

Take your time reflecting on the five questions of this section. When you've done this, consider:
- What was the most impactful thing you learned about yourself as an individual from the five reflection questions?

- What was the most surprising thing you learned about yourself as a manager about mental health at work from the five reflection questions?
- Are there any areas or roadblocks that you're now aware of that you need to work on?

Remember, you can't be expected to support a team member about mental health at work if you aren't comfortable with or give yourself permission to discuss it yourself.

Now that you've considered your views around mental health, and are aware of what may hold you back, let's delve into the actions you can take to:

- Set the tone that mental health is safe to talk about in your team, and
- Navigate these conversations in the moment as a manager.

HOW TO SET THE TONE

"The culture my manager was able to create was an openness around mental health. Having that role modeling set by him freed me to do the same thing for myself."
L, a Black female working in the consulting industry

Changing a workplace culture, even if just the micro-culture within one team or department, takes time.

As this book isn't about company-wide strategy, please try to look at this from the viewpoint of what you, as an individual, as a manager, can do for your team. If you happen to be the CEO or founder, then great – I would highly encourage you to tell the senior leaders and middle managers in your business to read this too, so they, and their teams, can benefit from the education with a blueprint for change.

Making changes to the tone and culture of a team are a *slow burn* and won't happen overnight. If you think about it, the culture you're in now took a certain amount of time to become that way, so it will take time to change too.

> *"Supporting mental health at work is a long game with results that will last for a long time. It's a culture shift in the office which can be scary, but it's something that's necessary to humanize your employees and make them feel like they're a part of something they want to be a part of."* E, a Caucasian female working in the tourism industry

This will be an iterative process. The size of your team, and even your company size and age can influence this process. Your microecosystem (team) has its own factors and the larger ecosystem (company) can impact your microecosystem. For example:

- A startup with 20 people will have a different journey than a Fortune 500 company with 2,000 employees.
- A new manager may face different challenges than a manager that has been there for decades.
- There will be different considerations between a large and a small team, and potentially a different rapport between manager and team members.
- Your starting point is your company's existing culture and values around mental health. This could range from mildly positive to extremely damaging to non-existent, and everything in between. Your starting point may determine the length of time it takes to see change.

Regardless of these factors, the most important thing is for you to remain open to trying different ideas to set the tone you want to create. These ideas include not only things you can do as a manager to set the tone, but ideas that you can encourage your team members to do with each other. Once you've set that tone, it will give the overt permission that your team members need.

TIP

You know your team (hopefully) better than other people in your company do. Take the guidance in this chapter and use what you feel would be best and *realistic* for your specific team or department. Regularly check in with your team to see how things are landing.

BUILD TRUST BY SHARING

When working to set the tone of mental health being safe to discuss in your team, you must think about one core thing: trust. Trust is *everything*. Without trust, you can't build anything else.

In Maslow's Hierarchy of Needs there are five levels to the pyramid (listing from base to peak): physiological, safety, love and belonging, self-esteem and confidence, and self-actualization. Without getting your needs met at the base, you can't move up the pyramid to get your next level of needs met, and so on and so forth until you reach the peak (and reach your full potential).[60] When people feel they can trust others, it builds feelings of social safety (level two). Trust amongst humans also creates a sense of belonging (level three).

Trust through belongingness *must be* met before people can reach their full potential. You may remember that in the roadblock of Your Self-Concept, we discussed the fear of being seen as different, an outsider or strange (page 77) due to mental health issues. Making people feel like they belong will break down that roadblock.

When we look at this from a manager's perspective, if your team members feel psychologically safe, this will hopefully lead them to feel more content at work, be more productive, and have a stronger connection to their peers and to you.

So trust is key. But how can you build it?

Humanize Yourself and Role Model

Organizational change consultant Gustavo Razzetti notes that *"Embracing vulnerability will not only show you are human, but also that you trust yourself and are confident to confront your own flaws."*[61]

Self-disclosure and showing vulnerability will help to dispel the roadblock of "leadership stoicism" (page 91) and is the best way to build trust. Sharing personal information (within your comfort levels, but you may need to give yourself a little nudge) about your fears, experiences, thoughts and feelings is a powerful tool in setting the tone for your team members that they can speak up about their own mental health or stress... because you are.

You can weave this into everyday conversations – mentioning your feelings or struggles in passing during a quick chat, in a team meeting, or any other time you feel it's appropriate. We'll get into how to make mental health conversations explicit in your team in a moment, but bringing it up unprompted has great effect.

What could this sound like?

Let's say you're chatting in a 1:1 with one of your team members and they asked how your weekend was, and you spent part of the weekend in bed because you've been struggling with clinical depression. You could say, *"My weekend was so-so, I've been feeling low lately, so I'm trying to focus on taking care of myself more these days."* Whether you actually share that you have a clinical condition is up to you, but by mentioning that you weren't feeling good emotionally, you've now signaled to your team member and set the precedent, at least casually in conversation, that it's a safe topic to discuss.

HR MANAGERS

If you work in Human Resources (HR), have a team reporting to you, and you want to share about *your* mental health with them (as discussed on page 141), you're in a really unique position. HR has been historically (unfairly) stereotyped as having to remain perpetually neutral in any work situation, maintaining the business' interests as the number one priority. (That doesn't sound very fair to the emotional wellbeing of those people working in HR.)

Thankfully, in recent years there has been a shift in the HR space to encourage HR professionals to talk about their own mental health within the companies they work for. To have an HR representative speak about their own mental health as an individual humanizes their role and may make it more likely for someone to seek guidance from that department. It can show your vulnerability and experiences as an individual and employee of the business, not as a *representative* of the business.

MITIGATE FEAR BY BEING EXPLICIT

The next step of setting the right tone is to dismantle any notion of fear in your team around discussing mental health. This fear may come from their own perceived fears, beliefs and past experiences (as discussed in Part 1), from your (or another manager's) previous actions, or if you've made them feel (intentionally or not) that they should be nervous to talk about their mental health. Everyone has their own reasons.

Some people will still be hesitant to chat with you about this topic because of the fact that you have general influence over whether or not they keep their job. Think about all of the fears we've already covered in this book about why people are afraid to speak about mental health at work. Those apply here *more than ever* when you sprinkle power dynamics on top of the situation.

Firstly, the act of sharing and humanizing yourself in day-to-day conversations will start to chip away at people's fears and negative beliefs around the potential outcomes of talking about mental health at work.

TIP

There is a *big difference* between having your team fear vs. respect you, but often the two are intertwined for a lot of employees. You need to actively work to mitigate fear, build trust and understanding in your team about psychological safety, and encourage discussions about mental health with you as their manager, and hopefully their team peers.

Secondly, often you need to just spell it out. Being explicit in what you say about mental health goes a long way to eradicate fears within your team, giving them clear permission to discuss it. And dispelling any preconceptions - head on.

Let's look at three practical ways you could do this.

Team Meeting Talking Point Option

Dedicate time in a team meeting to let people know that you as their leader are thinking about their mental health and want to make sure everyone knows they can come to you if and when they need to. The vibe you're going for is *option without obligation*. More details on specific steps to follow for this shortly.

Let them know that you:

- Genuinely care about mental health and are not just mentioning it as a tick-box exercise.
- Want to emphasize that you understand how important mental health is at work.
- Want to create a team environment where it's ok to talk about mental health, stress, or mental illness.
- Understand this is a personal topic, so there's no obligation to share, but that you want to let them know your door (physical or virtual) is always open.
- Don't know all the answers and need to hear what their needs are from them.

This would be a good opportunity to start that process through role modeling self-disclosure, participating in the conversation with them, about your own mental health (as we discussed above on page 178). If you're asking them to talk to you, you must talk to them. You can use the specific guidance in Chapter 6 when it comes to talking about *your* mental health.

Mention in a 1:1 Option

The above guidance also applies if you decide to raise the topic individually with your team members in a 1:1. With this option, make sure to explain to each of them that:

- You're addressing this topic with each person individually, so they know it's team-wide and not relegated to solely them.
- You're addressing it individually at first, before talking about it as a group.
- You want to be mindful of their individual needs and give them the space to discuss it privately with you.

If a mental health discussion results from that 1:1, revisit how to navigate this conversation in Chapter 7, and read the rest of this chapter for some suggested managerial approaches.

Call Out a Negative Discussion

You may also decide to be explicit about your advocacy around opening up constructive mental health discussions if an opportunity arises within a wider conversation. Let's say some assumptions or flippant comments around mental illness are being tossed around by a couple of people on a team call. As discussed in Part 1, commentary like this and misuse of language is a *big reason* that people are nervous to talk about mental health at work. There are a couple of ways you could address this. You can either:

- Privately message or speak with the two team members (individually or separately) to engage in a direct discussion about why what they said doesn't make people feel safe to talk about mental health – not in a punitive manner, but rather from a coaching for change manner (e.g. asking questions to understand *why* they said those things, and action-oriented questions about how they'll change their behavior going forward).
- Use it as a teachable moment live for the whole group, without making the offending persons feel like they're being publicly admonished. You could remind the group that talking about mental health is healthy, mental illness is common, and the team should do their part in the company to normalize this.

The focus of either option is making sure the team *pause*, think about the language they used, and understand that not only should they be more mindful of what they say, but also how they look at mental health and mental illness. This could also be a moment where you choose to role model by self-disclosing about your own mental health.

UNCOVER YOUR TEAM'S ROADBLOCKS

Every workplace and team will have their own dynamic and issues. In setting the right tone, it can help to examine the culture that already exists within your team – a mixture of individually held beliefs and workplace issues. By considering your team's biggest roadblocks, you'll be able to focus on removing them. This is a good time to refer back to Chapters 4 and 5.

The key here is *naming* what these roadblocks are for your team members and unpacking what's real versus perceived (e.g. based on actual experiences vs. private assumptions that have gone unchecked). As a reminder, below are some potential roadblocks to explore that may be preventing your team members from speaking up: within your team culture, or from their personal beliefs.

Roadblocks Within Your Team Culture
• A culture of wellbeing shaming
• Inflammatory or co-opting language that's used
• Compartmentalization culture
• Communication issues
• Management stoicism (recognizing you might be the issue)

Roadblocks Held Personally by Team Members
This is a harder one, but could bring in the task about finding out what someone else feels privately about mental health and mental illness based on their individual life experiences:

• Generational differences
• Gender-based emotion stereotypes
• Different ethnicities and religions within the team
• Experiences of past sharing that went poorly

TASK
Explore Your Team's Roadblocks

Setting the intention of this exercise is *crucial*. Don't spring this on your team live without context – big no-no. Remember, it's all about the *why*. This is an opportunity for you to tell your team members that this is important to explore and you want to give them the space to do this.

Typically, sending an email ahead of time to your team about *why* you're doing this exercise and your intended outcome (e.g. removing the roadblocks) will hopefully encourage people to speak up in the conversation in the moment. It's also useful in the email to let your team members know that if they're not comfortable to mention their roadblocks in front of the team, that they're welcome to email those to you ahead of time directly so you can be aware of what they are, but that you'll encourage them to try to participate in the exercise so everyone does their part. Let them know they don't need to share every single detail or a 15-year history about their roadblocks, but *some* contribution is important so there's reasonably equal participation from the whole team.

Have the team meeting with the purpose of naming what those roadblocks are, with the intention of seeing which ones can be removed, and the purpose of doing so: having constructive and supportive discussions about mental health at work. Emphasize that it's meant to be a constructive exercise for the team with the aim of getting everyone on the same page, and being conscious of each person's positions on the matter.

Ask your team a series of questions to determine what these roadblocks are (referring to Chapters 4 and 5 to give them some ideas). Encourage honesty without repercussion. Remember, this isn't group therapy, it's just opening up a constructive team conversation.

Some examples to guide your questions could be:

- Is it perceived that if someone vocalizes that they're stressed out that they "won't get ahead"? Debunk that immediately (e.g. let them know that isn't something they should be concerned about, because you as their manager wouldn't use mental health as a reason that they couldn't advance in their career).

- If it feels helpful or appropriate in the moment, ask your team if they feel potential generational definitions play a part in "what's appropriate to bring up at work".

Then – the important piece – ask them what would make them feel like those roadblocks have been removed. Keep in mind, *not every* roadblock can be removed, and in fact, some of those roadblocks may be slightly self-protective in nature. So, ask which roadblocks they want or are willing to have removed, and ask what you and each team member can do to contribute to this removal process (with specific examples, so you all know what it looks like in practice). Add any insight your team gives you into the picture you are building of your team's culture around mental health.

DOCUMENT YOUR TEAM'S STANCE ON MENTAL HEALTH

Through the tasks in this chapter so far, you'll have hopefully gathered a picture of what your team's culture is like, what their fears and roadblocks are, and made your stance on mental health explicitly clear.

Another positive step is to involve your team members to create a "team stance" on mental health at work – a mission statement of how the team collectively views mental health as a value at work, with specific team commitments around what this looks like in practice.

This can be a living document that all of you can craft and define collectively around how you all want to approach mental health in your team. Doing this may be useful, so your team members have a reference point to go back to around discussing mental health in the team. Take an approach that focuses on inclusion, cultivating empathy, and curiosity to learn others' stories. The task below will show you the steps you need to take with your team to form this document.

Please don't do this exercise until you've done some other groundwork to let the team know that this is a consistent topic that will be discussed in the team going forward, and you've given them an opportunity to unpack and discuss some of the roadblocks that may be in their way. These steps *are crucial* so people actually feel relatively comfortable and willing to participate in creating a team stance on mental health.

TASK
Create a Team Stance on Mental Health

Either schedule a team meeting, or dedicate time in a pre-existing team meeting with the agenda to create a team document on mental health. Allow for at least 15–20 minutes so it's not rushed.

Ask your team to attend the meeting ready to share their thoughts on what this team stance could be (e.g. words, phrases, sentiments) and that they're welcome to email you these in advance so you can aggregate everything into a document that the team can revise live. Hopefully, if you've put into practice the points of this chapter so far (and built trust and mitigated some fears), your team members will feel they can share with you in this forum.

Begin by asking your team broad questions such as:

- What does mental health mean to you?
- What does mental illness mean to you?
- Why is supporting mental health at work important to you as an individual?
- Why is supporting mental health at work important to our team?
- Why do you feel it's important to be supportive, or receive support, from your team peers or me as your manager around mental health?

Next, try and drill into what reasonable mental health support and understanding from colleagues may look like on a day-to-day basis, asking:

- What would empathy around mental health look like in practice toward each other, or from me as your manager?
- What can I do as your manager to reasonably support the mental health of this team? Day-to-day? In 1:1s?
- Can you think of any behaviors or actions within this team that may hinder constructive mental health discussions?

End by trying to gather consensus on your team's stance on mental health, by asking:

- What should our collective statement be around constructively discussing mental health in our team?
- What are our top five values when it comes to mental health at work? For example, empathy, seeking to understand, being inclusive.

Write up this document and upload it to a shared online folder that only your team has access to. It will live there and can be revised over time as needed.

Now you've taken practical steps to achieve an open and collaboratively agreed-upon tone around mental health in your team, and discussed your intentions with your team, let's move on to look at how to navigate a conversation around mental health. Specifically, between you as a line manager and your team member. Hopefully the steps you've already taken will lead to a few of these!

HOW TO HAVE CONVERSATIONS AS A LEADER/MANAGER

All of the conversation building blocks of Chapter 7 are still relevant to you. There are also a few nuanced items to highlight, in your role as a manager.

REMEMBER THE LIMITS OF YOUR ROLE

Be a great leader, but maintain *reasonable* boundaries. Remember the parameters and limits of your role (see page 139).

This one is particularly important because you sit in a position of advisory, influence and authority as this person's line manager. As such, especially for those people managers who are *very* empathetic, it can be a slippery slope from providing support in a professional context to feeling like you need to "fix" things or save them (gently remove the superhero cape please). Support your team members by directing them to the resources that can best help them.

In some cases, because of the role you hold, your team member may look to you for validation that how they're feeling is ok. Opening up this conversation between the two of you is absolutely the goal, but there's a difference between sharing and being supportive, and being a boss-turned-psychologist.

To check you're fulfilling your intended role, reflect internally on the following as the conversation unfolds:

- Is this just an "unloading" conversation with no need for further action?
- Would it be helpful to build-in a general wellbeing check-in during their weekly 1:1?
- Do they need to discuss changes to workload?
- Do they need to be connected to company resources or speak to HR?
- What do next steps look like – can we collaborate on what this means? (While you *are* their boss, and they may look to you for a steer on where to take the conversation next, first put the ball in their court and ask what feels like a useful next step.)

Remember, good helpers *ask questions and don't give advice.* And, good helpers enable people to self-manage and make positive decisions to help themselves when possible.

If for some reason you feel the dynamics of the conversation moving toward therapy territory (e.g. you can feel your team member becoming more dependent on you), a helpful way to navigate this is by letting your team member know that you truly appreciate them being open with you, and that you want to be supportive, but that ultimately you want to make sure they get the type of support that's actually going to be helpful for them on a deeper level (e.g. the EAP, speaking to a mental health counselor, etc.). *Do not* make it feel like you're "cutting them off", but more just giving a gentle reminder that it would be helpful for them to take advantage of the resources available to them that could help them more than you could as their boss.

GET TO KNOW YOUR TEAM MEMBERS' BASELINE

How would you know to check in with one of your team members if "they seemed off" if you didn't know what "off" looked like for them? I'm not saying to watch them like a hawk;

just pay attention. What does "good" look like for them? What does "bad" look like?

> *"Get to know someone's baseline. Awareness is observing. When you're talking to someone, don't just actively listen, actively watch too."* R, a Caucasian male lawyer

Here are a few simple ways to do this:

- Connect more often! Especially with our transition into remote work in recent years due to the pandemic, physically distanced doesn't have to mean interpersonally distanced.
- Ask them questions about who they are, their life, and their experiences. (Show genuine interest, so it doesn't come off like you're prying.)
- In a 1:1, you could ask (and don't forget to state why you're asking): *"So what do 'bad days' at work look like for you? As the team manager, it's good for me to be aware of this so I can be supportive."*

It's also important to remember that just because you see odd or different behavior from your team member doesn't mean that it's mental illness. It could be stress. They could be having an off day. You don't know the actual reason unless you ask. And, don't assume that because your team member is stressed out, or if they have a mental health condition, that they can't do their job. That's one of the key reasons people are afraid to speak up about mental health at work to their boss.

If your team member seems not to be thriving in their role (e.g. they're having trouble with tasks, it's stressing them out, or potentially triggering their mental health issues), then there's an opportunity to gain mutual understanding between the two of you on what's working, what's not, or if the role needs to be modified if possible.

Additionally, if your team member discloses to you that they do have a mental health condition, *do not* assume that *all* bad days that they have or behavior that seems off their baseline is because of their condition. It could be because of something totally unrelated. While it's good to be aware of their condition for when it is impacting them at work, be mindful that it's not always the reason for a struggle they may be having.

TIMING REALLY MATTERS

Do *not* choose to bring up your team member's mental health for the very first time during an annual review or any type of evaluation-focused meeting. Annual reviews can be stressful even for the most confident and well-developed employee, so bringing up their mental health for the first time *ever* during a review process will do exactly that – make them feel like their mental health *is under review*. Merging the two discussions also implies that you feel someone's mental health is directly related to their work evaluation. That's the opposite of what the aim here is.

The aim is to integrate discussions about mental health into the *everyday fabric* of your team discussions, not at points of evaluation that have to do with pay rises, performance enhancement and career progression. Of course, checking in on how the team member feels from a wellbeing perspective may be part of your annual review, as is common across a lot of companies – but don't pick that as the *first* time you're bringing it up.

Instead, find a moment where you can both speak candidly and without pressure, like a casual catch-up or 1:1. It may also be appropriate to make an in-the-moment observation (not in front of others) when the person is engaging in the behaviors that you're concerned about. If you do this, remember the question and observation techniques from page 144.

BE VERY CLEAR ON YOUR "WHY"

As this person's manager, you must make sure they understand you're coming from a genuine place of care, seeking to understand, and most importantly, that you're not coming from a threatening place (e.g. their job is safe).

Put yourself in your team member's position. If you were approached by your manager about the state of your mental health without explanation or context, there's a pretty good chance you'd be sweating bullets and assuming that your job was in jeopardy.

Afford this person the courtesy of explaining why you're speaking to them about what you've observed. In particular, if you've gotten to know their baseline, that helps explain why you've noticed they "haven't been themselves lately". Let them know you're trying to open up the lines of communication so they know that they can come to you as their manager if they need to.

Some helpful statements here could sound like:

- *"I know I'm your manager, but I do also care about how you're doing in general. I want you to feel like you can talk to me if you need to."*
- *"I've noticed that you've been unreachable some mornings in the past couple of weeks. That's really unlike you since you're usually pretty communicative all day. Is everything alright?"*
- *"I noticed that as we were talking about the X project, you seemed a bit overwhelmed – can you help me understand how you're feeling? Maybe we can work it out together."*

RESPECT THEIR BOUNDARIES

Just as you need to maintain reasonable boundaries within the limits of your supporting role, it's equally as important for you to remember that your employee needs to feel like they can maintain their boundaries and say "no" or "not yet" to you. If you're raising a concern with them about their mental health, you need to make it clear that they aren't obligated to share with you even though you sit in a position of authority. It's their personal information and up to them whether or not they want to share it with you.

RECOGNIZE THEIR COURAGE

A team member telling their manager that they're struggling with their mental health takes *serious* guts.

Remember all of the roadblocks of Chapters 4 and 5 about why people may feel worried to share with a manager? Fears such as not wanting to be seen as incapable or weak, prevented from advancement, or potentially get fired. Those are very real and valid concerns for some, particularly if those concerns came to fruition for them at past companies they worked at.

Commend them for their courage and let them know how appreciative you are as their manager that they felt comfortable opening up to you. Specify that you feel it's improved (not been a detriment to) your manager–supervisee relationship.

This can also be another opportunity for you to role model as a leader and open up about your own mental health, so they don't feel as though they're left out billowing in the winds of vulnerability. Use your discretion to work out if it's helpful to share (refer back to Chapter 7 about this); you don't want it to seem like you're making the discussion about you.

RESPECT PRIVACY AND CONFIDENTIALITY

I emphasized the importance of confidentiality in Chapters 6 and 7. Leader–team member confidentiality is *critical* in maintaining trust in this relationship. The last thing you want is a team member feeling like a person who sits in a position of authority is gossiping about them behind their back. Think of D's story on page 88 and how heartbreaking it was for him when his privacy was breached. It's imperative that you respect your team member's privacy and foster psychological safety as their leader.

SUICIDAL DISCLOSURE

If a team member discloses to you that they're feeling suicidal, you shouldn't deal with this alone as their manager. As we discussed in the last chapter (page 153), your number one priority becomes their safety and getting them connected to resources. Please enlist the help of emergency resources, your HR department, or other appropriate personnel in your organization on those emergency protocols. And work with the relevant HR or other personnel in your company to ensure a smooth re-entry for your team member back into work post-incident as necessary.

BE CLEAR ON PRACTICAL STEPS

Make sure you're both clear on any next steps from your conversation – especially with potential role changes or project logistics. Decide these steps together (ideally suggested by the team member), so it doesn't feel like you're making decisions for them.

- If they want to tell the team how they've been feeling, work with them to decide how and when they want to do this.
- If they need to make workload changes that affect other team members, get their consent that you can share at a *high level only* with the relevant members (and ensure those team members will also respect confidentiality).
- If they end up needing accommodations for a mental health condition, arrange a conversation with HR with their consent (or whoever has the responsibility for these HR matters within your organization).

You also don't want your team member to feel like you're watching them constantly *after* having a discussion about their mental health. They may assume you're seeing and treating them differently. Offer check-ins, if that's something they want, but don't hover. Put the offer out there, but let them tell you what they want going forward.

TASK
Have the Conversation with a Team Member

Prepare to have the conversation about mental health with one of your team members.

- Decide on the team member that you would like to speak with. (Not randomly, but with intention, e.g. one that you've already been meaning to speak to.)
- Consider why you feel you want to speak to this particular person, noting any observations you have made (to use within the conversation).
- Keep in mind the roadblocks that may come into play for your individual team member and team culture (from your task on page 184).
- Decide whether to start the conversation in a scheduled 1:1 or in a casual conversation.
- Follow the general conversation pointers from Chapter 7, and be sure to consider the special considerations your role as manager brings (in this chapter).

After the conversation, consider:

- How do you feel the conversation went?
- Do you feel the team member understood your "why"?
- Do you feel you responded well and asked the right questions?
- What would you like to improve upon next time?

CHAPTER SUMMARY

- Before you can talk about mental health at work with your team members, you must first check in with yourself. Reflect on your own perceptions or concerns about discussing mental health at work and shift those as needed.
- Set the tone that "mental health is safe to talk about" in your team by:
  - Building trust by sharing your story
  - Mitigating fear by being explicit about your objectives
  - Examining what may be hindering your team (roadblocks)
  - Defining your team's stance on mental health.
- When having mental health conversations with team members:
  - Be supportive, but maintain boundaries and remember your role.
  - Get to know your team members' baseline, so you can notice when something's off.
  - Don't assume mental illness or stress means they can't do their job.
  - Get your timing right: don't bring up mental health in an annual review for the first time.
  - Be clear about why you're bringing up mental health with a team member, so your intentions won't be misinterpreted.
  - Be ok if they don't want to discuss their mental health with you as their manager.
  - Respect their privacy, as you sit in a position of influence.
  - Be clear on potential next steps, and if it will impact other areas of your team.
  - Engage your resources, relevant colleagues and emergency protocols if your team member discloses suicidal thoughts.

PART 2 CONCLUSION

In the last few chapters, we've discussed the practicalities of mental health conversations in detail. There's one more area to consider: mental health at work during *really* tough times.

We'll be looking at three areas in particular: the impact of immense long-term stress, the mental health impact of COVID-19, and continued global racial injustice – complex, difficult, and necessary impacts to be aware of around the mental health at work conversation – regardless of where you sit in the business structure.

PART 3

WORKPLACE MENTAL HEALTH DURING TOUGH TIMES

9

THE EFFECTS OF IMMENSE STRESS

Whether it's an economic crisis, political unrest, natural disasters or other big current events, there's always something that's emotionally, financially, socially, or physically impacting people and potentially causing tremendous stress.

As you've learned throughout this book, people bring these stressors into work. Ongoing stressors that we react to with transient emotions and feelings, day in and day out. This is "normal life" as we know it.

But in recent years (and one year in particular), it's felt as though these external stressors have, for lack of better phrase, been put on steroids, and played out in a very particular way...

THE STRESS CRISIS OF 2020–2021

I'm writing this book amidst three generation-defining events. Many other important global events also occurred during this time period, but for the purpose of this book, it's important to focus on these three. Entire tomes could be written on these topics alone.

The COVID-19 pandemic: lockdown after lockdown. People losing their jobs from crippling economies. People getting sick, dying, and frivolously disagreeing on the necessity to wear masks and socially distance. Fights over toilet paper. Discrimination and direct violent acts toward people of Asian descent across the US and UK, because people were angry that COVID started in China. People denying COVID-19 even exists. Debates on the validity of the vaccine. Hopefully when this book is published, the immediate threat of the virus will be somewhat controlled. However, the effects of the pandemic will be around for a long time.

"*I can't breathe!*": the last words of George Floyd as he was being slowly killed by the police. A racial trauma that shook the world. The Black Lives Matter (BLM) resurgence in response to this moment, captured on social media. The subsequent wave of global protests and riots. People taking to the streets in droves demanding change worldwide toward the treatment of and marginalization of Black people. The continued and blatant policy brutality toward the Black community, despite the cries of millions for it to stop. People still delusionally denying that racism exists.

The insurrection attack on the US Capitol in Washington, D.C. – fueled by President Trump himself – where rioters took over the Capitol with relative ease, in protest of the administration change to President Joseph Biden. A frightening reality that most doubted could ever occur. And yet, it did, with an alarming disparity in how unharmed the violent rioters were. A stark contrast to the peaceful BLM demonstrators who on many other occasions were greeted with intolerance and indignity by police authorities. Shock waves were felt around the world.

With the turn the world has taken, writing a book about mental health at work during the time of palpable international turmoil, without discussing the long-term mental health impact of these specific elements, would be an incomplete work.

I'm not an expert on the mental health impact from an epidemiological point of view in a pandemic, nor am I an expert on the mental health impact of racism and racially based marginalization (especially as I'm conscious that I'm a Caucasian woman who hasn't encountered discrimination based on the color of my skin).

However, while these factors aren't the core focus of the book, their impact needs to be addressed with regards to the mental health at work impact in today's global society, and how that's brought into workplace conversations.

ORGANISMS EXPERIENCING GARGANTUAN LEVELS OF STRESS, ANGER AND FEAR

If there was ever an opportunity to understand the meaning of the full spectrum of emotions (page 5) and Dr. Willcox's Feelings Wheel, with its 78 options, it's now. Ups and downs, fear, anxiety, uncertainty, frustration, anger (so much anger), and every other component of the cocktail of emotions.

However, in these three generation-defining events that have occurred, I don't solely see people getting angry and disagreeing with each other. What I also see is organisms that are struggling to adapt to an unstable, changing and volatile ecosystem.

Some organisms are afraid and hunkering down. Some are reacting angrily, in denial, trying to keep the ecosystem from changing. Some are moving with the flow. Some are trying to construct the new ecosystem in a helpful way. The changing of this ecosystem has brought out the best in some and the worst in others; it's unified some and divided others. It's had a massive impact on our mental health and become a significant complication (and therefore roadblock to overcome) in the mental health conversation.

And of course, these feelings, triggers, fears and opinions are brought into work. How could I talk about what people emotionally bring into work without addressing what's physically keeping them out of work buildings and what plagues their minds intermittently throughout the day?

The COVID-19 pandemic and the resulting global economic downturn. Social isolation. Mass layoffs and furloughs, job uncertainty, survivor's guilt, illness and death. Social divisiveness in how people did or didn't help stop the spread of the virus.

The unjust racially motivated (seemingly never ending) murders committed by police officers in the United States of citizens. The explosive reaction to this racial injustice sent the globe into a totally justified reactive wave of putting the proverbial foot down against continued racial injustice – everywhere.

Protests around the world. The spark of a global discussion. Statues of slave owners and known racists were torn down. People flooded the streets, marching, to put an end to an overdue wound on human history.

The global frustration and anger toward individuals, companies, and governments who didn't take this social movement seriously. Who didn't show up for their employees. Who got their PR department to "say the right things", but didn't actually *do* anything.

The international shock of the "response" to the Capitol attack, despite the fact that government authorities were warned *ahead of time* that something like this could occur. Advanced warnings were given by the FBI that this would come, and yet wafer-thin protections were put in place and government agencies were prevented from acting, because the previous Administration declined to take the threat seriously, and stoked the fire. And so, they came in droves, violently.

Some guards at the Capitol even *welcomed* some of the rioters by opening up the partition rails and letting the rioters walk around the Capitol building freely. Rioters who pepper-sprayed and physically beat police officers, broke windows of the building, carried the Confederate flag in the halls (something that had never happened in the entire history in the US), and even took selfies with security guards. White supremacy at its finest. The nation was thankful for the police officers and guards who actually tried to stop the attack, who sacrificed their own physical safety to do so, to protect the Capitol and the elected officials who were being ushered off to safety while hearing death threats from the crowd. A stark juxtaposition, and heavy add-on, to an already inflamed and necessary conversation about racial inequity.

2020 and 2021 put us all in a pressure cooker, laced with intense emotions that put us into survival mode for *far* too long.

EFFECTS ON MENTAL HEALTH

To say the effects have been significant is an understatement. Beyond the massive financial and physical impacts, the mental impact has been *astronomically significant.*

As I write this book, the negative trend data has started pouring in of the mental health impact from COVID-19 and from the willful neglect of racial inequality. This data shows both the social impact – and the impact at work. As I pivoted my business overnight to be 100% remote, requests from companies started flooding in on how to tackle these difficult topics with their staff and leaders from an emotional point of view.

So, within this book we must look at these three generation-defining events individually and how they intersect with mental health at work, and those conversations, in a significant way.

Having an awareness of what people mentally and experientially bring into work has always been important, but is more crucial now than ever.

From 2020 on, mental health at work *must account for and be empathetic toward* what people are bringing into work from the impact of the systemic, interpersonal, and internalized racism, and the ongoing impact of COVID-19. Going forward, you can't talk about mental health at work without thinking of those things.

This book's main focus is on what you can *do as an individual* to further these conversations. Obviously, you alone can't eradicate these heavy hitting issues. What you can do, and what is within your control, is to broaden your awareness of their impact and create a safe space for conversations around these topics. Keeping with the theme of this book, doing your part will make an impact on those around you.

In chapter 10 we'll look at the mental health impact of COVID-19 and explore the ramifications of the pandemic. We'll look at what people may be emotionally bringing into work with them, key considerations in how the pandemic has changed workplace practices around mental health at work, and how colleagues, and managers, can best support and interact with one another.

In chapter 11 we'll take a deep dive into the mental health impact of continued racial inequity, key considerations for what the Black community may be emotionally bringing into work with them, and look at how to create space for these crucial discussions.

CHAPTER SUMMARY

- The COVID-19 pandemic and continued blatant racial inequity are two significant stressors that have impacted the world on a global scale.
- We are organisms under a state of distress, with each organism reacting in a different way, with different emotions, thoughts, and behaviors.
- Social division has become a massive stressor.
- These key stressors are being brought into the workplace, and they must be addressed.
- You can make an impact through awareness and creating space.

10

COVID-19 AND
MENTAL HEALTH

The way I look at the mental health impact from COVID-19 is this: we're all organisms with a rapidly changing environment that experienced a major threat. This put us all in a *massive* long-term state of distress. An invisible threat to our livelihood that could literally have taken our breath away, circulating the globe at an alarming rate. What's worse is that the threat of this illness was brought to us by our own species (once it jumped from animals).

To survive a threat, organisms under duress do one thing: enter survival mode.

When organisms are in survival mode, it's natural to have reactionary symptoms from encountering a stressful stimulus, and as a result, sometimes display noticeable variations in behavior. Even though we're higher functioning organisms, beings with large frontal lobes in our brains that give us the ability to speak, think, innovate, and create, we're no exception to the animal kingdom when it comes to feeling like our lives are being threatened. When animals feel threatened, their emotions and behaviors change. This can manifest in many different ways, but with one end goal: to maintain safety. In this case, from each other.

The main themes that have driven the mental health impact thus far are:

- Fear of the unknown
- Social isolation

- The loss of loved ones
- Uncertainty of the future
- Fear of physical harm from the illness
- The loss of "normal life and activities"

We'll unpack several of these themes in this chapter and the impact they've had – personally and in the workplace.

THE COVID-19 IMPACT

It's not a question of *if* mental health has been impacted by COVID-19. It's a question of *how severe* the impact is and how we deal with it.

THE MENTAL HEALTH EFFECT IN BRIEF

The biggest trends and studies at the time of writing this book have shown the emotional health results from the above causes worldwide to have been: an increase in chronic stress, anxiety, suicide, depression, insomnia, trouble concentrating, trouble with memory, PTSD, trauma, substance abuse, feelings of loss, bereavement, relapses in addictions, hypochondriasis (health anxiety), and domestic violence.

The rise in hypochondriasis is particularly relevant because COVID-19 had so many different symptoms that at the slightest moment of any physical discomfort or abnormality, many people jumped to thinking it was due to COVID-19.

It will take years until we know the full extent of COVID-19's impact, but to give you a data point-in-time snapshot:

- A report by the global database management company Oracle, released in October 2020, showed that the COVID-19 pandemic has created the most stressful year in its employees' lives, ever, and has negatively affected the mental health of 78% of its global workforce.[62]

- The US Centers for Disease Control and Prevention reported that, compared to the same period in 2019, the rates of anxiety and depression in the US significantly increased to alarming rates – they have quadrupled.[63]
- A study published by the American Psychosomatic Society showed that repetitive lockdowns in the UK have led to a significant increase in depressive, anxiety, and insomnia symptoms.[64]
- Mental Health Foundation UK is leading a long-term UK-wide study on the mental health impact from the pandemic, and has already published statistics on nine waves of effects.[65]

With the sheer gravity and frustratingly long duration of the COVID-19 global pandemic, it's understandable that mental health condition diagnoses have risen, and behaviors have changed. The human brain and body are incredibly resilient... to a point. Even those who are well equipped to cope have their limits. Sadly, as a result of COVID-19, I'm predicting that the often-touted statistic of 1 in 4 people having a diagnosed mental health condition globally may be revised to 1 in 3, or even 1 in 2. Only time will tell.

THE IMPACT OF THE LOSS OF SOCIAL CONTACT

We are social creatures and have survived as a species by relying on each other. From a macro level, we work together to create a stable economy and maintain some semblance of law and order and so forth. However, even though we needed to "work together" to overcome COVID-19 through collective social distancing measures and adherence to government guidelines, we also developed a pronounced fear of each other. Our social unity fractured under the threat of illness and death, giving birth to the survival of the individual and not the collective.

On a micro level, during the lockdown phases of COVID-19, we lost the most basic form of social bonding – being around, and making physical contact with, one another. A hug, a handhold, a kiss, even just sitting next to one another. To fear this basic social contact was *incredibly* impactful on people's psyche, making them feel isolated and disconnected from one another. Looking at the neuroscience, losing this ability to touch one another means we don't get the serotonin and dopamine boost gained from physical touch, which helps to regulate moods and reduce stress.

Institutions including the Texas Medical Center have noted the mental and physical health impact of "touch deprivation", which include increased stress, depression and anxiety, higher levels of cortisol (the stress hormone) which activates our body's flight-or-fight response, increased heart rate, blood pressure, muscle tension and a decrease in immune response.[66] Psychiatrist Dr. Asim Shah put the impact into very simple terms: *"When someone is [touch] starved, it's like someone who is starved for food. They want to eat, but they can't. Their psyche and their body want to touch someone, but they can't do it because of the fear associated with, in this case, the pandemic."*[67]

RE-ENTRY ANXIETY

A new psychological phenomenon developed as a result of fear of the virus and social interaction that psychologists have dubbed "re-entry anxiety". Psychologist Lily Brown, director of the Center for the Treatment and Study of Anxiety at the University of Pennsylvania, highlighted two types of re-entry anxiety:

- The lurking fear of catching COVID-19 ("I'm terrified of getting sick")
- The fear of resuming socializing ("I'm afraid to be around people again")[68]

A June 2020 *Time* magazine article noted that people felt terrified to go out in public for fear of catching COVID-19, but also didn't know how much longer they could cope being cooped up at home.[69]

Guidance to help people soothe their re-entry anxiety started pouring out from the psychology community and media outlets. While people were encouraged to stay safe, take baby steps when resuming safe social interactions and seek counselling for their mental health, people were still understandably frightened and wary. For those who already had mental health conditions, the pandemic has proven to be quite triggering for some of them, despite the coping techniques they may have learned in therapy. Especially due to the fact that the virus mutated into far more infectious variants and there were questions around the effectiveness of vaccines against those variants.

PEOPLE STILL FEEL LIKE THEY CAN'T TALK ABOUT MENTAL HEALTH

Earlier, I mentioned one of the reasons why people are afraid to talk about their mental health at work is because they don't want to seem like they "can't handle" difficult situations. Believe it or not, in the time of COVID-19, that still applied, and if anything, exacerbated this issue for some.

Despite the globally recognized mental health impact, some studies showed that workers remained hesitant to speak to their manager or people in the company about their mental health, for fear that they would be seen like they couldn't cope and perform, and that they may be replaced. This was particularly visible in companies that, prior to the pandemic, hadn't given the social permission to discuss this topic.

A study by Paychex around mental health at work during COVID-19 found that out of the 1,017 full-time employees surveyed, 54% said they felt uncomfortable talking to their managers and supervisors about mental health; 30% of respondents feared that discussing their mental health could lead to being fired or furloughed; and 29% thought discussing their issues could cost them a promotion.[70]

A RISE IN IMPOSTER SYNDROME WHILE WORKING FROM HOME

Not only did many remain nervous to discuss the pandemic's impact on their mental health at work, but studies also showed that some people worried about their job safety and performance as a result of working from home, which is a practice set to continue beyond the initial crisis.

Working at home and away from your normal office environment can lead to:

- A lack of in-person positive interactions with managers (which can make you question your worth)
- A lack of "being seen" at work (which can lead to fears of perceived lower productivity and a pressure to over-perform)
- Isolation (which increases opportunity for negative self-talk, with no one to sense-check or silence that inner critic).

You can see that these factors can trigger self-doubt and negativity in some about their performance, and can lead to Imposter Syndrome (IS). While Imposter Syndrome is *not* a clinical mental health condition, it can still be very emotionally distressing for people to experience.

Feelings of IS tend to manifest as:

- Irrational self-doubt
- Feelings of inadequacy about your job performance
- Feelings of intellectual fraudulence
- Attributing success solely to external factors
- Discomfort and deflection when receiving compliments
- Maintaining these feelings in the face of success due to your own hard work
- Either trying to over-prove yourself or withdrawing from opportunities so people don't "find you out"

In short, people with IS feel like they're a fraud.

First coined in the 1970s, IS isn't a new phenomenon. A 2019 Hub Events survey asked 1,000 adults in the UK about Imposter Syndrome and found that a shocking 80% of men and 90% of women experience IS at work.[71] So, what happened to the people who already experience IS, once COVID-19 hit? The pandemic heightened those feelings of inadequacy for many.

When shifting to working from home, people already trying to over-prove themselves at work had a tough challenge ahead of them: their thought process went to being "out of sight and out of mind", and a fear that they would *definitely* show their co-workers that they "weren't good at their job and were expendable".

LOSS OF CONCENTRATION

Issues in concentration and memory have been shown to be affected by chronic stress. It's left a literal impact on the brain. Even before the pandemic began, a study conducted by the National Institutes of Health (NIH) in February of 2020 showed chronic stress makes us understimulated, which can be just as stressful as being overstimulated. Now add the pandemic on top of that.

There are consequences for this. A *Washington Post* article summarized the study:

"Chronic stress is potentially harmful to the brain, in part because it leads to a persistent increase in the level of the stress hormones cortisol and norepinephrine. We know from animal and human studies that chronic elevation of cortisol can cause shrinkage of neurons in the hippocampus – a brain region that is critical to learning and memory." [72]

I call this "pandemic brain".

KEY CONSIDERATIONS

COVID-19 literally overnight fundamentally changed social interactions and working practices around the globe for many. For those who went virtual, people grappled with working from home indefinitely and attempting to set up a home office alongside their partner, potentially with children to homeschool too. For others, they faced being ordered to continue to come into work, despite worrying publicized data that the virus wasn't under control and not having enough access to personal protective equipment.

There has almost been a forced blending of work and life. The once-separate, compartmentalized environments are now integrated (even for those who didn't want them to be). Imagine how hard that was, and may continue to be for those set on compartmentalizing work and life.

With the effects of COVID-19 in mind, and hopefully a post-pandemic period on the horizon, every organization will have its own challenges in helping employees to navigate this complex changing environment: The duty of care to ensure that employees have a safe and healthy working environment, even if that's remotely distributed; through policy, flexibility, and updating of work practices, and most importantly, through *conversations*.

You know what I'm going to say here.

You *can* have an impact as an individual, through the conversations you have, through the example you set by talking about the hard and uncomfortable stuff. Everything we've talked about in the previous chapters on mental health conversations still applies, but there are a few COVID-19 considerations to keep in mind. Within your conversations, consider:

- Focusing on the positives and finding the silver linings (*not* toxic positivity!)
- Acknowledging the bad stuff
- The importance of staying connected and supporting each other in a virtual environment
- The importance of being flexible with each other
- Keeping up to date on the changing landscape around mental health at work

FIND THE POSITIVES AND RECOGNIZE THE MOMENTS

Remind your colleagues (and yourself) that, believe it or not, there are positives to come out of the pandemic – the silver linings.

COVID-19, alongside the sadness, stress and death that has occurred, has also given us some morsels of hope and moments of appreciation – personally and at work. Note that this is *not* the toxic positivity mentioned on page 36. Acknowledging the bad stuff (coming next) is still very much needed.

The massive trauma and invisible enemy that is COVID-19 forced society to work together, support one another, and forced us into a new pace of life. Consider the following positives that have come out of the pandemic:

Personal Positives
- Many of us benefitted from having calendars somewhat simplified, to slow down and just "be".
- In the face of huge stress, it was an opportunity to appreciate the small things in life.
- It caused many to focus on and appreciate the relationships we care deeply about.
- It helped us to be more compassionate to each other.

Workplace Positives
- Companies that hadn't yet started talking about mental health in the workplace began talking about it (because people couldn't continue on without addressing it).
- Managers had the opportunity to begin conversations around mental health, with the socially acceptable "in" of *"How are you coping in the lockdown?"*
- Many people who have a mental health condition that's better managed at home benefitted from the home-working changes.
- Those with a lengthy commute had more time for self-care or family time.
- Some were able to build team rapport, with the extra focus on good communication and added glimpse into others' home lives.

Try to recognize moments with your colleagues or team members where it would be useful to highlight these silver linings. It could bring a moment of relief.

TIP

Please be mindful to *not* mention these silver linings to a colleague who lost someone to COVID-19.

ACKNOWLEDGE THE BAD STUFF

While considering the positives does help get through some of the tough times, it's equally as important to acknowledge the bad things too. If we didn't, we would be no better than the toxic positivity movement discussed in Part 1. Here, we'll consider what you can do to help your colleagues or team members acknowledge the bad stuff.

Acknowledge Fears and Feelings

- Acknowledge how your colleagues or team members feel and don't tell them "not to worry" – even if you're trying to help them feel better.
- Remember, COVID-19 has turned the world on its head and the psychological impact of this is palpable. A lack of acknowledgment of how they feel can be just as painful as the feelings themselves.
- Acknowledge the reality of the situation, while providing *realistic* hope.

Focus on What You Can Control

- Be encouraging and help colleagues focus on what they *can* control and influence. Try saying something like: *"Yes, the situation is s**t, and you have the right to feel that way. In an effort to help take the sting off, what can you focus on at work or at home where you have some control?"*
- Ask your colleagues what gives them a realistic sense of comfort or safety, and suggest they focus on creating those conditions for themselves, whether they're at home or when they're out.

Normalize Experiencing Negative Emotions

- People who tend to feel guilty for displaying negative emotions in general may still feel guilty for these emotions... even during a pandemic.
- People who might usually be on "an even keel" may be surprised with the depth of negative emotions they are experiencing.
- Normalize how someone is feeling and that it's understandable to feel that way. That it's ok to not feel ok. Refer to page 151 on how to do this.
- Reference that we're all under distress and that we're all trying to cope and navigate the complex changing environment.

SURVIVOR'S GUILT

Medical News Today explained "survivor's guilt" in association with PTSD, particularly when a person has feelings of guilt because they survived a life-threatening situation when others didn't – particularly traumatic events (e.g. war, cancer, natural disasters, etc.).[73] This is true for those who caught COVID-19, and survived, while a friend or family member didn't. Or for those who weren't exposed when others were.

There's also been a wave of people experiencing "survivor's guilt" at work during the mass furloughs and redundancies that have occurred as a result of the pandemic. Even though being furloughed or made redundant isn't a "life-threatening situation", it's still a situation where the people who still have jobs *survived* in a way that their colleagues didn't. Guilt arises from remaining employed when their colleagues weren't so lucky.

For people you think are experiencing survivor's guilt (and potentially for yourself):

- Remind them that their feelings are valid. Remind them that everyone is trying to find their way through this, and peaks and troughs are normal.
- Remind them that their life doesn't need to be destroyed for them to experience negative emotions, feel stress, or be worried.
- Encourage your colleagues or team members to be kinder to themselves.
- Encourage them to be as flexible with themselves as they (hopefully) are with others.
- Most importantly, if their feelings become too strong to manage, to reach out for mental health support from a therapist or other available resources.

THE IMPORTANCE OF STAYING CONNECTED AND SUPPORTING EACH OTHER IN A VIRTUAL ENVIRONMENT

As we've already covered, it can be difficult for colleagues or managers to know someone needs help unless they explain what's going on and what they need – this is especially true if you consider the virtual environment many people are now working in, and will probably continue to work in long past the pandemic. Home working has become the new norm for many companies, along with the work flexibility and office rent savings that come along with it.

The option of a quick mental health check-in chat is important now more than ever. As I mentioned on page 190, physically distancing doesn't mean you need to be interpersonally distanced. Use technology to your advantage and check in on how your colleague is doing, especially if they've had the onset of new mental health symptoms or potentially a mental health condition. Do your part.

Take the opportunity to share how the pandemic impacted you. What's been the hardest for you? Share it with your colleagues or team members. Hearing your experiences may give them the permission they need to disclose how they're feeling.

VIRTUAL PRESENTEEISM

Something to be mindful of when staying connected via technology is the pressure of "virtual presenteeism". This is the expectation for people to be *constantly* connected and reachable all the time. To reply to an email immediately, for fear of being thought to be slacking off.

The last thing you want is for someone to feel pressured to immediately respond to a mental health check-in. So, keep people's schedules in mind and remember that they can answer in their own time. Send the message and leave it in their court.

BE FLEXIBLE WITH EACH OTHER

Everyone has experienced the hardships of a pandemic in different ways, ways we wouldn't know unless we asked. Be authentically curious and ask your colleagues how they're doing and what challenges the pandemic has brought up for them... and really mean it.

Remember that everyone has their own unique life, home set-up, finances, etc. For some, it can be comforting to be at home. For others, it can be triggering, a struggle, and potentially mentally unhealthy for them. Everyone copes in their own way and we can't judge each other for that.

When it comes to planning for meetings, deadlines, keeping in touch, and other work-related items, be flexible where possible. Let them know that it's ok if one of the balls falls out of the air from time to time – because it happens to *everyone*.

FOR MANAGERS, ROLE MODELING IS CRUCIAL NOW MORE THAN EVER

The key considerations in this chapter are crucial for you as a manager and should be considered alongside the specific guidance of Chapter 8. A few key pointers:

- As a leader, check in regularly, and with authenticity.
- Where you can, create space to really connect with your team, not just on their work product.
- Self-disclosure from you as their leader is really powerful, so your team knows it's ok for them to open up too.
- Let them know, as a team, that you'll navigate together how to do their best work as a team and support each other as a team.

TASK
Keep Connections Consistent and Purposeful

Come up with a realistic (and not overwhelming) cadence to commit to checking in with your colleagues or direct reports about how they are handling the pandemic's effect on their life. And, hold yourself to it.

- Create the space and make the time.
- Ask what their biggest struggle has been.
- Ask how they're taking care of themselves.
- Ask if they're doing alright.

You have all the tools you need in the previous several chapters to equip you for these discussions. This might be the catalyst you need.

CHAPTER SUMMARY

- During COVID-19 we have been organisms under a state of distress. The impact has been significant: physically, psychologically, behaviorally, financially, socially and professionally.
- The psychological impact is clear through many themes, including the loss of physical contact, the development of re-entry anxiety, and a rise in Imposter Syndrome.
- Some people *still* feel like they can't talk about mental health at work.
- What you can do: remember the silver linings, acknowledge the bad stuff, stay connected in a virtual environment, and be flexible with each other.

By the time you read this, even more data and information will have been published about the COVID-19 impact on mental health, so please use this as a point-in-time assessment and keep adding to your knowledge on the pandemic's impact as it develops.

11

THE CONTINUED MENTAL HEALTH IMPACT OF RACIAL INEQUALITY

We need to take a look at one more topic: continued racial inequality and how it impacts mental health at work and the conversations we have.

More specifically, having an awareness of what people in the Black community are experiencing and emotionally bringing into work with them, showing that you truly acknowledge their (and their community's) experiences.

It took me a long time to write this chapter. I asked myself: how can I make sure to explain this in a way that's meaningful and helpful from a high level in *just one* chapter? Can I give this topic the thoroughness it deserves? Can I write about something objectively when it's so politically sensitive and I have a very clear opinion on it? Can I write about this as a Caucasian Jewish woman? (I hugely grappled with this one). Unlike the Black community, I've had the luxury of wearing my diversity on the inside. And while I've experienced direct anti-Semitism that has been very painful, as have my family members, and lost nearly the entire side of my father's family in the Holocaust, I'll still never know what it's like to be treated differently at work, racially profiled on the street, treated with indignity by police officers, or have consistent fear and discrimination based on the color of my skin. I'm also conscious that I've been fortunate to feel safe to discuss my experiences around anti-Semitism in the workplace because it's a topic that is deemed more "socially acceptable" for some reason (e.g. people can seemingly tolerate it more than talking about racism).

If you have experienced any of the moments of discrimination I listed above, words can't express how frustrated and angry I am that this happened to you.

Whoever you are, you will approach this topic with your own idea on how to further the conversation around the mental health impact of racism within your work environment, and I encourage you to share these with your colleagues where possible.

Whatever your cultural or ethnic makeup is, I highly encourage you to sit with any discomfort you may experience while reading this chapter. To seek to understand (or reflect on if it's happened to you) the mental health impact of experiencing racism. To continue to learn about the emotional trauma that people in the Black community have been experiencing for a *really* long time, and how it's staring them in the face today in a way that's painful and unsustainable. To understand the rightful anger and sometimes feelings of helplessness that the Black community feels from the willful ignorance they encounter. And most importantly, to learn how you can create space for these conversations at work, just as you would for any other human who has gone through something so stressful, sustained, and horrific.

Please note: I'm conscious that using the term "race" has become somewhat outdated, inherently implying division; and it would be more appropriate to use the term ethnicity. However, in some places in this chapter I use this term as it relates to academic terminology or was used in certain lived experience stories, both of which are quoted verbatim.

THE SPECIFIC LENS

I am approaching this topic specifically from a mental health at work conversation perspective, with the aim of understanding just a few points within this complex topic, and giving you a few ways to open up conversations in this space. To start small, and most importantly, to *action* your learning. I'm also approaching this topic using data, research and the lived experience of my interviewees, in an attempt to ensure the chapter includes a number of relevant voices.

I hope you'll take from this chapter:

- Key considerations: building an awareness of the emotional health stressors that the Black community faces, and the pain and frustration when these aren't transparently discussed in the workplace.
- The importance of creating space for learning and discussion on this topic.
- Practical tips you can act on.

As you've learned throughout this book, we bring all of ourselves to work – body, mind and experiences. For those who have an extra layer of experiential trauma based on the color of their skin, they're bringing that in with them to work. The Black community, and other communities of color, have experienced all the stressors we've talked about in this book – *plus* multiple forms of racism.

I want to clearly acknowledge that the racism that other people of color experience is *just as important* and should also be discussed. Experiencing racist behavior is painful and unacceptable. It's also important to recognize that the racism that people experience is *very personal,* and each community's experiences are unique.

This chapter will focus on the Black community due to the litany of long-time police brutality that boiled over from the death of George Floyd (amongst many others) and the specific time period. This specifically affected the Black community and sparked a *global* conversation around racism toward Black people worldwide in a massively significant way. This *does not* discount the racism that other people of color have experienced. Those are just as horrible and deserve their own attention to unpack, which would honestly require an entire additional book (if not more). Fitting this segment into one chapter on its own was one of the largest challenges I experienced when writing this book.

Please note: the following information and ways to address this are solely focused on the *emotional health* aspect, not the entirety of the issue as a whole. The Diversity, Equality, and Inclusion (DEI) professionals in your organization, your HR department, your senior leaders, or consultants who may come in to speak at your company, will have specialized knowledge on this area on a larger scale or can deploy a DEI strategy aimed at creating change and advocacy from a company-wide culture-shift perspective. This chapter is meant to give you a few ways to look at this social issue from a mental health impact perspective and how to be mindful of these factors in mental health at work conversations with your colleagues from the Black community.

Let's look at the concepts, data, and stories to help you understand these considerations.

KEY CONSIDERATIONS

"I think the Black Lives Matter movement has contributed to opening up the larger discussion of racially based collective trauma and how that negatively impacts mental health within the community. But, I do not believe I can discuss the mental health impact of the Black Lives Matter movement at work because the topic generally would not come up in conversation. The atmosphere in the office does tend to be solemn when news breaks of another shooting of an unarmed Black person, but beyond that,

it is not a topic of conversation." K, a mixed-background female (Black and Caucasian) working in administrative support

THE HUMAN PAIN OF NOT FEELING SEEN, OF FEELING ABANDONED

In discussions with my interviewees who are part of the Black community, L and K both offered perspectives that struck me to the core.

L explained that one of the most harmful impacts on the mental health of Black people in the workplace is when they feel *abandoned* by their employer. Especially when most of the senior leadership positions are held by people who are Caucasian. Black people not only feel that their workplace doesn't stand up for what's right (through public statements, or even internal statements at the company), but that what's going on is not even acknowledged in conversation. This is for a sad and fixable reason: awkwardness and not knowing how to approach it.

The polar opposite approach also happens, when companies or leaders ask Black employees to become the poster children for their public statements, so the company can show that they've "done their part". Or companies, leaders or colleagues look to those employees to wholly teach them about the entire social issue, without doing their own homework.

In June 2020, *Fortune* magazine featured an article where numerous people in the Black community were interviewed about what it's like to work as a Black person in corporate America. A woman named Kelli shared how the above felt for her:

"I am white enough that people are comfortable with me, as long as I don't call too much attention to my blackness. I am seen as black when they need me to shed light on the 'Black experience.'"[74]

Inclusive culture advocate and Talent & People professional Madison Butler speaks openly on social media about workplace diversity and inclusion. She is honest in all the ways people need to hear, regardless of their comfort level; blasting from a megaphone that racism *is* a workplace issue.

Throughout the resurgence of the BLM movement, Madison crafted post after post of education, perspective and pleas to the general public to understand what people in the Black community need to feel emotionally supported at work. She wrote one particular post that truly summed up the mental health impact that people in the Black community have had and are continuing to shoulder. It's something that everyone in the workplace should read. In August 2020, Madison wrote:

"Dear Black people,
It's been a hard week. It's been a hard month. It's been a hard year.
It's been a hard century. It has been hard.
Take care of yourselves, not just today but every day.
It's ok to unplug. It's ok to binge Netflix and eat snacks. It's ok to do whatever you want.
It's ok to block that bully from your hometown. It's ok to turn off the news.
It's ok to focus on your family.
It's ok if all you do today is just breathe. It feels like we're constantly holding our breath waiting for the next tragedy, the next hashtag, the next trending topic.
We are more than that, we have always been more than that. So, I hope today, you just breathe."[75]

Dr. Brittany Linton, a clinical psychologist in California and a Black woman, wrote about this internal struggle and feelings of frustration that Black Americans in particular experience around the lack of substantive discussion about mental health in the workplace from these specific elements.

"A colleague asked me recently, 'How are you doing – really?' Between the dramatic life shifts from the coronavirus pandemic, changing work expectations, the pre-existing plague of racism now at the forefront of awareness, mental gymnastics to see if my White leaders and co-workers would supportively respond to anti-racism discussions, and significant stress from personal concerns.

I feel like 2020 is winning the race and my emotional reserve batteries are running low. My Black community and I have been hit hard.

I couldn't mask my pain – and didn't desire to – in the middle of the workday. I candidly shared, 'I'm struggling'. Let's pause to consider what it means to be Black at work in America.

The professional standards Black Americans are expected to uphold at work often require extensive limiting of emotional expression, among other double standards, to navigate systemic racism in the workplace.

In fact, many Black employees cannot authentically show up at work as full versions of themselves without facing professional ramifications, adding another layer of stress on top of normal job demands. This balancing act in the workplace is rarely properly addressed by employer-provided mental wellbeing programs. This experience only intensifies with an ongoing normative productivity burden following exposure to horrific racist events, which can go ignored or minimized in workplaces..." [76]

CNN published an article in the wake of the global conversation, particularly focusing on racism toward Black Britons in the UK.

More specifically, the article focused on how racism in the UK is alive and well, but that it hasn't gotten "as much press" as it has in the US, and the BLM movement in the US has sparked the desire for it to be finally dealt with (a relevant example being how the Windrush generation was dealt with).[77] Someone quoted in the article summed it up quite well saying, *"The greatest trick racism ever pulled was convincing England it doesn't exist."*

FEELING SILENCED – A CONSTANT PRESSURE TO "KEEP IT TOGETHER"

How unfair is it that if someone experiences racism outside of work – whether personally or witnessing family or friends be discriminated against – that they then feel they can't talk about it at work because *people would feel uncomfortable*? Or if they did speak up, they might be labeled as "angry" based on a ridiculous stereotype that was designed to silence them? Someone experiences a traumatic event... but talking about it is taboo.

If this has happened to you, perhaps you felt like you couldn't speak up at work. How many times did you feel like that? That you couldn't vocalize how you felt because the vibe around you was that your colleagues or boss just couldn't handle it? Or you were scared it would go wrong? I'm conscious that recalling this may be potentially painful, but I appreciate your willingness to do so for the purposes of reflection.

The silence from others is horrific.

And a long-term wound has been ripped open, yet again, after seeing a number of horrific poignant police brutality events toward the Black community in 2020, that showed the world how systemic racism and marginalization is very much alive and well, that many people in the Black community suffer in silence as their multitude of vocal pleas for change, no matter the approach, have gone unanswered. To add insult to injury, the attack on the US Capitol and the soft treatment of the rioters threw the continued inequity in the Black community's face even more.

The expectation at work remains for *many* people in the Black community from their colleagues or employer: "we" don't feel we need to talk about "that" at work. That's a "personal" issue. The corporate steer: keep it together and put on a happy face. This is *unconscionable*, cruel and ridiculous.

> "The stress of being Black man in corporate America means we can't have the full range of emotions. We can only be happy – never angry." Bernard, Fortune magazine[78]

L, a Black woman, shared her experiences and fears with me in detail, and how she acted around her colleagues so as to not make them feel "uncomfortable":

> "Early in my career, I kept quiet. There was fear there. I was conscious of the narrative of the 'angry black woman'. I was conscious early in my career that I didn't want that label, so I kept quiet. I took great pride in being someone people relied on. I got stuff done. I thought the worst thing I could do back then was to not be the person that people could rely on. I felt that's what would have happened had I spoken up. People would think I wasn't the person they could rely on, that I was just the angry black woman.
>
> Why should people have to silence themselves from the indignities they have been through? It's a ticking time bomb.
>
> Look at the masks we wear at work, and different environments we interact with on a day-to-day basis. My fear is that people of color wear those masks every

single day, especially at work, because they don't want to be labeled as disruptive or disloyal. They don't want to be labeled as the troublemaker, because ultimately if they get that label, they're asked to leave that business. They're no longer a part of the circle of trust. They are being asked to put on a mask, bite their tongue, to not say the things that need to be said. That their masks need to stay firmly in place... for them to survive.

If you're being asked to wear this mask and hide who you are as a person, what does that do to you? If you have to create these characters, then who are you? Who do people see? Who are you internally? These different characters will fracture you and can only negatively impact someone's mental health.

You get pulled in so many different directions. How on earth could you be at peace with yourself and have stability in your mental health?

Think about the people who are on the streets day in day out fighting for equality and a better experience. Think of the people who are wondering if it's their day to be bundled into a van or be kidnapped on the street. That fear is there. It's present. The fear of not being able to be yourself, not being able to speak and have a voice, and people just denying your experience because they don't have a clue. Their discomfort trumps your ability to be yourself and share your experience. That's why I think it's a timebomb. I hope there will be a change." L, a Black female working in the consulting industry

MINORITY STRESS AND RACE-BASED TRAUMATIC STRESS

Traumatic events people experience due to the color of their skin absolutely impact their mental health.

Being discriminated against for the color of your skin is so prominent and long standing that there are psychological terms for it – minority stress and race-based traumatic stress.

In Chapter 4 we discussed the outside-of-work stressors, mental health struggles, experiences, and opinions that people bring into work with them. Here's another heavy layer that people in the Black community experience, and bring to work. And not being able to talk about it at work? You bet your ass that this is an inside-of-work stressor, just like we discussed in Chapter 5.

Minority Stress

Minority stress refers to the stress that people of marginalized groups experience because of the discrimination and prejudice they encounter. An article in *Healthline* on minority stress recognized its health impact, and the anxiety that comes from experiencing everyday acts of discrimination, victimization, and microaggression.[79]

When we think about some of the stories shared in Chapter 4 about the historical trend in the Black community to *not* talk about mental health, even though this has changed in recent years, it's now clear that many people in the community have reached a breaking point (if they hadn't already) where they can't stay silent about racism's mental health impact anymore – to each other or to people in other communities.

Author Lola Jaye wrote a piece for the BBC in August 2020 about how the emotional and physical toll and trauma of racism has taken its toll on Black people:

"The experience of racism – both direct and indirect in the form of micro-aggressions or exposure to racism via the media – can have a devastating effect on the mental health of black people. This effect – known as

"racial trauma" – can lead to depression, hypervigilance, chronic stress and fatigue, bodily inflammation and symptoms similar to post traumatic stress disorder... If the knee on the neck of George Floyd was symbolic of how countless black people have felt and experienced life for centuries, it has brought many deep-rooted emotions to the surface."[80]

Race-based Traumatic Stress

Along the same vein, but centered more on specific trauma and PTSD, is race-based traumatic stress. The impact of this on mental health is significant and must be taken into account – the individual trauma mark that's left, and the pain of feeling the collective-trauma of a community.

Associate Professor of Psychology at Huston-Tillotson University, Dr. Andrea Holman, published an article about race-based traumatic stress specifically within the Black community which stated the importance of emotional self-care for those who experience it. Dr. Holman explained that this specific kind of stress is defined as an emotional injury that's motivated by hate or fear of a person or group of people as a result of their race (or racism) that can: overwhelm a person's capacity to cope, cause bodily harm or threatens one's life integrity, and cause fear, helplessness, or a sense of horror. Dr. Holman noted:

"Research shows that this stress can leave African Americans with physiological and psychological symptoms resembling post-traumatic stress disorder, or PTSD. Unfortunately, these types of emotional injuries occur with disheartening regularity and over time, can create chronic stress."[81]

SYSTEMIC, INTERPERSONAL, AND INTERNALIZED RACISM

All forms of racism are horrid, but it's important to delineate that there is more than one kind that people can experience.

Dr. Angela Neal-Barnett, a professor of Psychological Sciences at Kent State University who directs the Program for Research on Anxiety Disorders among African-Americans, wrote a piece for the *Harvard Business Review* on how organizations can support the mental health of their Black employees. She noted that it's important to recognize that people in the Black community can experience *three* distinct kinds of racism, all of which have different impacts, but that overall, racism is, in fact, trauma – the emotional distress we feel after encountering an awful or potentially life-threatening event. She noted that each form of racism is its own chronic stressor for Black people.

The three types and their impacts are:

- *Systemic racism*: experienced when ideologies, institutions and policies operate to produce racial and ethnic inequality.
- *Interpersonal racism*: involves two or more people and can be manifested through bigotry, bias, prejudice and microaggressions.
- *Internalized racism:* the acceptance of negative stereotypes and societal beliefs about one's racial group.

Dr. Neal-Barnett puts the emotional impact poignantly:

"The unrelenting series of events Black Americans have witnessed before and after the killing of George Floyd is racial trauma. Most Black Americans, regardless of education, socioeconomic status, or job title, experience

one or more forms of racism every day. But with the placement of a knee on George Floyd's neck, racism shifted from a chronic stressor to a trauma trigger." [82]

This trauma was felt on a global scale and was uncovered through important conversations in global, national and local discussions.

As we've discussed throughout this book, each person's experience is unique, and you should never assume you know how someone is feeling solely based on their cultural or ethnic makeup or what you have read. But, it's important to build the awareness of how it *could* be, how it *could* feel, and what people in a certain community may be shouldering depending on their experiences – and the level of frustration they feel with the mistreatment of their community, and potentially themselves.

THE IMPORTANCE OF CREATING SPACE FOR LEARNING AND DISCUSSION

Please try to sit with any discomfort around discussing this topic, including if you're discussing something that's happened to you, and remember that there is growth in discomfort – on all sides of the conversation.

Whether you're from a different community and you're seeking to understand, or sharing what's happened to you if you're a part of the Black community, both sides of the conversation are crucial. It's helpful and necessary to open up this conversation so the specific emotional toll on the Black community can be accounted for in the mental health at work discussion.

I went through this journey myself, seeking to understand how I could best support and acknowledge the emotional experiences and mental health impact of professional colleagues and friends who are part of the Black community, and more specifically surrounding the horrendous events of

2020 and early 2021. How could I be mindful, how could I be an ally, how could I make my individual contribution to shifting the narrative? (Part of which was the inclusion of this topic in this book.)

I sought to learn if my friends and colleagues were comfortable to share. I listened to personal stories. I learned that there are a wide variety of experiences and opinions in the community, and to take each story as that: the story of that unique person.

Create the space. Continue the learning. Have the conversation and decide how you want to contribute to it in an authentic and empathic way.

Many people in the Black community have had repetitive life experiences from systemic racism that have caused anguish, frustration and emotional pain. Just as you would have empathy and create space for someone to talk about what's going on for them emotionally when it comes to other life experiences, this should be no different, and should be at *their* pace and comfort level. And, if this happened to you, I hope you will create this space for yourself to talk about it at work. Your story *matters* and people can *learn* from it.

FEAR OF SAYING THE "WRONG THING"

Just as some people may have potential discomfort around discussing mental health or mental illness, ethnicity can be in that taboo topic grouping for some people too.

This is a complex subject that many avoid talking about because they "don't want to say the wrong thing". It's ok to be worried about saying the wrong thing, especially if you're well intended and want to be supportive. What's *not* ok is saying *nothing*. Not here, in my opinion, sorry.

It is very possible to say the wrong thing, when trying to be supportive and identify with what someone is going through. Comparing, for example, racial discrimination to gender discrimination.

Is gender a barrier at work and sometimes socially? Absolutely.

Does gender make someone get blanketly other'd at work or labeled with a racist archetype? Nope.

While both are a struggle for each respective group, the experience is unique and different, and shouldn't be compared.

In Lola Jaye's article about the intersection between race and mental health, she wrote about not denying someone the opportunity to share their experience because of *your own* discomfort. Not to say things like, "you don't see color, you just see them for who they are" as a way of trying to be supportive. This minimizes their experience and dismisses their perspective.

What can you do to ensure you don't say the wrong thing? Educate yourself. Ask people in the community about the *realistic* and *informed* way to look at the subject. I'm not saying you'll get it right all the time – we all make mistakes.

> *"People get stuck. They fear that the discussion will become a confrontation, that they will say something to offend 'the other'. They fear that because you can't walk in their shoes, you can't empathize. Actually you can, but it has to come from a place of genuine curiosity. If you are genuine in your intentions, educate yourself. That's where you start."* L, a Black female working in the consulting industry

The thing is, saying nothing is just as bad as saying the wrong thing. And, being silent is complacence toward the narrative not moving forward and opening up the conversation further.

So, how do you overcome this fear? In short, educate yourself so you have the knowledge to be informed and not ignorant. Seek to understand. Be curious. Don't make assumptions. Sit with the discomfort, learn from it. Realize that this topic, too, sits within the mental health umbrella, which absolutely *is* a workplace issue.

WHAT YOU CAN DO

If you're a leader, manager or CEO, while you don't need to be the be-all and end-all diversity and inclusion expert, you *do* have the responsibility as a leader (and social responsibility as a person) to understand the mental health impact of racism and the toll it's taking on your team members in the Black community.

If you're an employee, again here you don't need to be an expert, but you do have the responsibility to be an informed person, just as you would hope your colleagues would be about something significant and well-known that you're emotionally bringing into work with you.

SHARE YOUR EXPERIENCES

If you have a story to share from your experiences in the Black community, decide if you want to share, with whom, what you want them to learn, how to best support you, and what you're looking to get out of the conversation. It's helpful to revisit Chapter 6 for the building blocks of having this conversation.

If you're a manager at your company and are a part of the Black community, remember from Chapter 8: you're not expected to be a stoic, unemotional leader. If you've been affected by something you've experienced or witnessed happening to your community, it's good to share this if you want to. Vocalize to your team that you're processing what's happened and the impact it's had on you (based on the level to which you're comfortable sharing). Normalize the discussion.

SEEK TO UNDERSTAND AND SUPPORT

All of the information on supporting someone at work still applies here, whether it's a colleague or supervisee.

If you're seeking to learn about this topic from a colleague or team member, be sure to:

- Create space for honest discussion.
- Create psychological safety around discussing the topic.
- Offer genuine support as an option, not an obligation.
- Be ok with no and understand that they may not want to speak with you about it.
- Don't assume you understand how they feel.
- Normalize the conversation in a group setting – seize the moments to change the narrative and role model to your colleagues that this is a topic that's very much on the table.

While there must be broad, sweeping change at an organizational level throughout every company (and no organization is exempt), you can do your part through providing emotional support on a conversational level and creating psychological safety around the topic for your colleagues in the Black community.

If there was ever a time to show that you genuinely care (if you haven't before), now would be the time. Please be *authentic* in how you do this, don't be a band-wagoner and don't pressurize. You're engaging in this conversation because you *want* to and *value* its importance.

AS A MANAGER
Create Space
If you're a manager, just as you're working to create space to talk about mental health in general in your team, this also means creating a safe space to acknowledge the mental health impact of racism.

Dr. Brittany Linton, the psychologist we heard from on page 228 gave a very clear piece of guidance to managers on how they can best support their team members in the Black community, particularly after they've witnessed a socially traumatic event targeted at them or their community:

"It's important for managers to stay aligned, connected, and prepared to respond to Black team member needs. Team leaders are positioned to have the most direct influence on work demands and routine interaction with Black employees. Staying emotionally attuned by routinely checking in allows managers to both convey empathy and provide flexible instrumental support when needed, such as capacity for team members to carry out work tasks and adjust workload expectations."[83]

Create the space for your team members to say that they don't feel ok, if they feel traumatized, and to voice their needs. Don't make this forced or awkward, but rather that you as a leader recognize the importance of acknowledging those events and bringing the discussion out into the open.

Acknowledge the Impact

As with "acknowledging the bad stuff" around COVID-19, this *absolutely* applies here too.

Dr. Neal-Barnett gives some direction to leaders on how to support the emotional health of Black employees during these extraordinarily painful times:

"Start by acknowledging that racism impacts Black staff emotionally, mentally, and physically. Understand that when Black employees tell you 'We are exhausted,' 'We are tired,' or 'We are in no mood to interact with white people,' what is really being said is, 'We are in distress, we are traumatized, and we need a safe space within this organization to come together as Black people.'"[84]

Give your team members from the Black community the time and space for self-care as and when they need it. The emotional drain they may be going through is something you may never be able to relate to, but you *can* relate to the feelings of needing a mental break. Be an empathetic and compassionate leader who recognizes individual human experience and gives the acknowledgment and care that deserves.

Dr. Neal-Barnett also highlighted the power of listening and action in showing authentic care (something we've spoken a *lot* about in this book). I encourage you to heed and act on her words:

> *"Listen to what your Black employees are saying and advocate for the suggested changes. Do not limit listening to town halls or organization-wide meetings. Listen at lunch, listen at work, listen after work, and acknowledge and convert the ideas and recommendations you hear into action."*[85]

Enlist Resources and Your Support Network

Remember that you as a leader don't need to be the expert on racially based trauma, but as a manager you do need to acknowledge its existence, and its impact on your team members from the Black community. You also don't need to provide this support alone. Engage your network and resources. Just as with issues around mental health or mental illness, it's not your job to fix everything.

What *is* your job is having your team members from the Black community know that they can discuss how they're feeling with you if they want to, knowing what resources are available, and making sure they have access to those resources.

TIP

Change is coming slowly – and you're a part of that. You can do *your part*. You can find the moments to listen. You can find the moments to create space. You can find moments to understand. You can find the moments to act.

TASK
Educate, Listen, Then Act

This task is open ended. Please begin, or continue, to educate yourself beyond this book on the mental health impact of racism. There are resources listed at the back of this book that will help to continue your education.

Act by starting conversations, and listening. Explain that you're trying to learn more so you can do your part and that you're open to a steer on how to effectively and authentically do this. Explain your statement of intention: to be supportive and genuinely understand.

Act by sharing your story.

Remember, this book is about conversations. Equip yourself for *this* aspect of the mental health at work conversation. From the guidance in Part 2, you have the language and tools you need to seek to understand – or, to be understood, heard, and seen.

CHAPTER SUMMARY

- The Black community has been through their own unique set of racially based emotional stressors – and these are brought into work. Build an awareness of these stressors, and the pain and frustration when these aren't transparently discussed in the workplace.
- These stressors include, but are not limited to: feeling silenced and abandoned, pressure to "keep it together at work", minority stress, race-based traumatic stress, and three kinds of racism (systemic, interpersonal and internalized).
- If you have a story to share, please consider sharing with your colleagues so they can learn.

- Seek to understand and normalize conversations around racism.
- Create space for learning and discussion at work, because it's very much a part of the mental health at work conversation.
- Enlist resources and a support network in your effort to educate yourself fully.

A FINAL NOTE

What Will Your Impact Be?

You're not a grain of sand in an ocean – you're a rock being thrown into a lake. You will make ripples.

Even though you're just one person, what you do affects people around you. More than you know.

How big an impact you make is ultimately up to you, but you do need to play your part in the mental health at work movement toward change.

The more people that do this in the workplace, the quicker change will come. Current and future generations will benefit from how we've worked together to change this workplace narrative, now. I believe that discussions of general mental health and also mental illness will become just as common in the fabric of workplace discussions as talking about physical health, current events, or family.

Be a part of the change. Don't just observe from the sidelines.

It's ok to be nervous, concerned that you may say the wrong thing or do the wrong thing. You're human. However, let me end with the words of psychologist Dr. David Gilovich, as he explores the actions we do or don't take in life:

"In the short term, people regret their actions more than inactions... But in the long term, the inaction regrets stick around longer."[86]

Please follow his words. Action this education. Do something with what you've read. And, encourage other people to do it too.

Thank you for reading this, and good luck! I'm excited – and I hope you are too – for the impact you'll have.

ACKNOWLEDGMENTS

This book only came to fruition because of the invaluable influence of the people I know and have met along the way, in this gloriously imperfect journey called life. In particular, there are specific people I want to thank.

To my husband, Matt, words can't express how much I appreciate you. Your counsel, tough love, feedback (even when I didn't want it) and empathy. Thank you for perpetually being in my corner, keeping my inner critic at bay, and standing by my side whether I was on my knees, wavering, or flying. I couldn't have written this without you.

To my parents, for encouraging me to do the work that I love, with passion and purpose. Thank you for drilling into my head that I should always strive to be someone who could make a positive impact on the world. I don't know anyone who works harder than the both of you. Thank you for giving me the genetics and the inner strength so I could do the same. Dad, thank you for encouraging me throughout the years to become the second author in our family. Mom, thank you for making me feel grounded and motivated when I was being hard on myself, and for always saying, "Go Bimpa!"

To my brother and sister, just like our parents, your tenacity and passion in your respective fields have always inspired me. Sandy, thank you for your cheerleading during this process. Mark, thank you for the big brother pep talk at the start of my writing journey.

To my interviewees who shared their stories for this book, you brought this piece of work to life. Thank you for your bravery, honesty and willingness to contribute to this project.

Your experiences will touch the hearts and minds of many. Please know how much I appreciate you.

To my graduate school professors, former clinical colleagues and supervisors, thank you for teaching me about the human condition, the full spectrum that is mental health and mental illness, and how to best help people help themselves. I wouldn't have become the professional I am today without your guidance and constructive criticism.

To my colleagues and mentors that I've worked with in the organizational psychology field, thank you for encouraging me to grow in this space and to focus on my specific passion area. It's led me to blend my former clinical life with my current organizational work – and I can't thank you enough for helping me move toward the niche that I was meant to do. Thank you for your role in this.

To my editors, Jo and Beth, thank you for making sure I created something practical and useful, not just educational. Your steers and feedback were priceless. Thank you for giving me the opportunity to create this book and helping me to achieve one of my biggest professional dreams.

To my supportive friends all around the world who encouraged me week after week and month after month to keep writing. You helped me to keep going when I really struggled. Thank you for being awesome.

Last, but certainly not least, to all of the people who have attended my keynotes, lectures, webinars, workshops, panels, interviews, and now... my readers. You are the reason that these changes *will* be possible. I couldn't do what I do without all of you being willing to do it with me. Thank you for caring. Thank you for taking action.

ENDNOTES

1   *What is Mental Health?* US Department of Health & Human Services, 2020. Retrieved from: https://www.mentalhealth.gov/basics/what-is-mental-health

2   Wilcom, Dr. G. *The Feeling Wheel*, The Gottman Institute, 1982. Retrieved from: https://www.gottman.com/blog/printable-feeling-wheel

3   *Mental Illness – Overview*, Mayo Clinic. Retrieved from: https://www.mayoclinic.org/diseases-conditions/mental-illness/symptoms-causes/syc-20374968

4   The *World Health Report 2001: Mental Disorders Affect One in Four People,* World Health Organization, September 2001. Retrieved from: https://www.who.int/whr/2001/media_centre/press_release/en

5   *Mental Health Problems – an Introduction,* Mind UK, October 2017. Retrieved from: https://www.mind.org.uk/information-support/types-of-mental-health-problems/mental-health-problems-introduction/causes

6   *Learn About Mental Health*, Centers for Disease Control and Prevention. Retrieved from: https://www.cdc.gov/mentalhealth/learn/index.htm

7   *Types of Mental Illness*, healthdirect, November 2018. Retrieved from: https://www.healthdirect.gov.au/types-of-mental-illness

8   *How to Manage Stress*, Mind UK. Retrieved from: https://www.mind.org.uk/information-support/types-of-mental-health-problems/stress/dealing-with-pressure

9   Salahi, L. *Catherine Zeta-Jones Sheds Light on Bipolar II Disorder*, ABC News, April 2011. Retrieved from: https://abcnews.go.com/Health/BipolarDisorder/catherine-zeta-jones-sheds-light-bipolar-disorder/story?id=13373202

10 Preston, A. *Astronaut Buzz Aldrin on Battling Depression, Alcoholism, and Why Mars is the Next Frontier,* The Telegraph,

June 2017. Retrieved from: https://www.telegraph.co.uk/science/0/astronaut-buzz-aldrin-battling-depression-alcoholism-mars-next

11 Bhandari, Dr. S. *Celebrities With Bipolar Disorder*, May 2019. Retrieved from: https://www.webmd.com/bipolar-disorder/ss/slideshow-celebrities-bipolar-disorder

12 Romeo Dallaire bibliography, Romeo Dallaire. Retrieved from: https://www.romeodallaire.com

13 Grant, J. *We Applaud These Black Celebs For Helping to Erase Mental Health Stigmas With Their Testimonies*, Essence, May 2019. Retrieved from: https://www.essence.com/lifestyle/health-wellness/black-celebs-help-erase-mental-health-stigmas-encourage-therapy

14 Farreras, I. G. *History of Mental Illness*, 2020. Retrieved from: https://nobaproject.com/modules/history-of-mental-illness

15 Ibid

16 *Mental Health in Schools*. National Alliance for Mental Illness. Retrieved from: https://www.nami.org/Advocacy/Policy-Priorities/Intervene-Early/Mental-Health-in-Schools

17 Mental Health Innovation Network. Mental Health Research UK. Retrieved from: https://www.mhinnovation.net/organisations/mental-health-research-uk

18 Chiu, A. *Time to Ditch 'Toxic Positivity,' Experts Say: 'It's ok not to be ok'*, The Washington Post, August 2020. Retrieved from: https://www.washingtonpost.com/lifestyle/wellness/toxic-positivity-mental-health-covid/2020/08/19/5dff8d16-e0c8-11ea-8181-606e603bb1c4_story.html

19 Torres, M. *5 Signs You're Experiencing Toxic Positivity At Work*, HuffPost, December 2020. Retrieved from: https://www.huffpost.com/entry/signs-experiencing-toxic-positivity-at-work_l_5fc7cedc5b640945e52ce30

20 Derickson, E. *How to Avoid Toxic Positivity*, TalkSpace, November 2020. Retrieved from: https://www.facebook.com/Talkspacetherapy/photos/pcb.3775884692461989/3775884619128663

21 Brüssow, H. *What is Health?* Microbial Biotechnology, US National Library of Medicine National Institutes of Health, July

2013. Retrieved from: https://www.ncbi.nlm.nih.gov/pmc/articles/PMC3917469

22 *Mental Health Matters: 8 Stigmatizing Phrases to Stop Using*, GoodTherapy. Retrieved from: https://www.goodtherapy.org/blog/mental-health-matters-8-stigmatizing-phrases-to-stop-using-050715

23 Greenwood, K. and Maughan, V. *Research: People Want Their Employers to Talk About Mental Health*, Harvard Business Review, October 2019. Retrieved from: https://hbr.org/2019/10/research-people-want-their-employers-to-talk-about-mental-health

24 Ibid

25 Oaklander, M. *Millennial Employees Are Getting Companies to Radically Rethink Workers' Mental Health*, Time, January 2020. Retrieved from: https://time.com/5764680/mental-health-at-work

26 Ibid

27 Brescoll, V. *Leading with their hearts? How gender stereotypes of emotion lead to biased evaluations of female leaders*, Science Direct, April 2016. Retrieved from: https://www.sciencedirect.com/science/article/pii/S1048984316000151

28 Ibid

29 Young, Dr. J. *Women and Mental Illness*, Psychology Today, April 2015. Retrieved from: https://www.psychologytoday.com/us/blog/when-your-adult-child-breaks-your-heart/201504/women-and-mental-illness

30 *Men and mental health*, Mental Health Foundation. Retrieved from: https://www.mentalhealth.org.uk/a-to-z/m/men-and-mental-health

31 Ibid endnote 29

32 Schumacher, H. *Why more men than women die by suicide*, BBC, March 2019. Retrieved from: https://www.bbc.com/future/article/20190313-why-more-men-kill-themselves-than-women

33 Malanda, T. *How depression has never been an African disease*, The Standard, 2014. Retrieved from: https://www.standardmedia.co.ke/entertainment/crazy-monday/2000131772/how-depression-has-never-been-an-african-disease

34 Bell, J. *The hidden face of mental health in the Middle East*, Arab News, May 2019. Retrieved from: https://www.arabnews. com/node/1496661/middle-east

35 Ibid

36 *Black/African American*, National Alliance on Mental Illness. Retrieved from: nami.org/Your-Journey/Identity-and-Cultural-Dimensions/Black-African-American

37 Tanap, R. *Why Asian-Americans and Pacific Islanders Don't go to Therapy*, National Alliance on Mental Illness, July 2019. Retrieved from: https://www.nami.org/Blogs/NAMI-Blog/July-2019/Why-Asian-Americans-and-Pacific-Islanders-Don-t-go-to-Therapy

38 Cruz, A. *Poor Mental Health, an Obstacle to Development in Latin America*, The World Bank, July 2015. Retrieved from: https://www.worldbank.org/en/news/feature/2015/07/13/bad-mental-health-obstacle-development-latin-america

39 Gberie, L. *Mental Illness; Invisible but devastating*, The United Nations, March 2017. Retrieved from: https://www.un.org/africarenewal/magazine/december-2016-march-2017/mental-illness-invisible-devastating

40 Mental Health Innovation Network. Retrieved from: https://www.mhinnovation.net/innovations/mental-health-system-reform-brazil

41 Moreira-Almeida, A., Neto F.L., and Koenig, H. *Religiousness and mental health: A review*. Brazilian Journal of Psychiatry. August 2006. Retrieved from: https://www.scielo.br/scielo.php?pid=S1516-44462006000300018&script=sci_arttext

42 Ivanov, A. and Mitchell, C. *Counseling and Russian Culture*, Counseling Today, April 2016. Retrieved from: https://ct.counseling.org/2016/04/counseling-and-russian-culture/

43 Wesselmann, E.D. and Graziano, W.G. *Sinful and/or Possessed? Religious Beliefs and Mental Illness Stigma*. Journal of Social and Clinical Psychology, April 2010. Retrieved from: https://guilfordjournals.com/doi/pdf/10.1521/jscp.2010.29.4.402

44 Rutgers University. *Mental health stigma, fueled by religious belief, may prevent Latinos from seeking help*, Medical Xpress,

April 2019. Retrieved from: https://medicalxpress.com/
news/2019-04-mental-health-stigma-fueled-religious.html

45 Saleh, Dr. N. *How the Stigma of Mental Health Is Spread by
Mass Media*, verywellmind, June 2020. Retrieved from: https://
www.verywellmind.com/mental-health-stigmas-in-mass-
media-4153888

46 Costello, Dr. A.K. *What TV Gets Wrong About Mental Illness*,
Northwestern Medicine. Retrieved from: https://www.nm.org/
healthbeat/healthy-tips/emotional-health/what-tv-gets-wrong-
about-mental-illness

47 Srivastava, K., Chaudhury, S., Bhat, P.S., and Mujawar, S. *Media
and mental health*, Industrial Psychiatry Journal, US National
Library of Medicine, National Institutes of Health, January 2018.
Retrieved from: https://www.ncbi.nlm.nih.gov/pmc/articles/
PMC6198586

48 Mcleod, Saul. *Carl Rogers*, SimplyPsychology, 2014. Retrieved
from: https://www.simplypsychology.org/carl-rogers.html

49 Lewis, C. *Mental Health in the Workplace Across the
Generations*, Aon. Retrieved from: https://www.aon.com/
unitedkingdom/employee-benefits/news/articles/mental-health-
in-the-workplace-generations.jsp

50 *What is psychological safety and why is it the key to great
teamwork?* Impraise. Retrieved from: https://www.impraise.com/
blog/what-is-psychological-safety-and-why-is-it-the-key-to-great-
teamwork

51 Pelletier, P. A. *Bullying at work: an ethical and leadership
dilemma for project managers.* Paper presented at PMI Global
Congress 2015–EMEA, London, England. Newtown Square, PA:
Project Management Institute. Retrieved from: https://www.pmi.
org/learning/library/bullying-at-work-9642

52 Dolezal, L. and Lyons, B. *Health-related shame: an affective
determinant of health?* Medical Humanities Volume 42,
Issue 4, June 2017. Retrieved from: https://mh.bmj.com/
content/43/4/257

53 *Faces of Depression: Philip Burguieres*, PBS. Retrieved from: http://
www.pbs.org/wgbh/takeonestep/depression/faces-philip.html

54 Saltzman, J. *CEOs and entrepreneurs, we need to talk about your mental health*, Fast Company, November 2018. Retrieved from: https://www.fastcompany.com/90269284/ceos-and-entrepreneurs-we-need-to-talk-about-your-mental-health

55 Fisher, J. *The Truth About Leadership and Mental Health*, Thrive Global, May 2019. Retrieved from: https://thriveglobal.com/stories/leadership-and-mental-health-challenges

56 Miller, D.C. *4 Lessons I Learned Coping With Depression in the C-Suite*, Entrepreneur.com, July 2016. Retrieved from: https://www.entrepreneur.com/article/277858

57 *Albert Mehrabian – Nonverbal Communication Thinker*, The British Library, Retrieved from: https://www.bl.uk/people/albert-mehrabian#

58 *Client-centered therapy*, Harvard Medical School & Harvard Health Publishing, January 2006. Retrieved from: https://www.health.harvard.edu/newsletter_article/Client-centered_therapy

59 Murphy Jr., B. *People Who Give Advice Like This Have Very Low Emotional Intelligence*. Inc.com, July 2020. Retrieved from: https://www.inc.com/bill-murphy-jr/people-who-give-advice-like-this-have-very-low-emotional-intelligence.html

60 Mcleod, S. *Maslow's Hierarchy of Needs*, Simply Psychology, March 2020. Originally created by Abraham Maslow, *A Theory of Human Motivation* in Psychological Review in 1943. Retrieved from: https://www.simplypsychology.org/maslow.html

61 Razzetti, G. *How Unwritten Rules Shape Your Culture*, Thrive Global, January 2018. Retrieved from: https://thriveglobal.com/stories/how-unwritten-rules-shape-your-culture-unlike-your-vision

62 *AI @ Work Study 2020: As Uncertainty Remains, Anxiety and Stress Reach a Tipping Point at Work*, Oracle, October 2020. Retrieved from: https://www.oracle.com/human-capital-management/ai-at-work

63 Czeisler, M.E., Lane, R.I., Petrosky, Dr. E., Wiley, Dr. J.F., Christensen, A., Njai, Dr. R., Weaver, Dr. M.D., Robbins, Dr. R., Facer-Childs, Dr. E.R., Barger, Dr. L.K., Czeisler, Dr. C.A., Howard, Dr. M.E. and Rajaratnam, Dr. S.M.W. *Mental Health, Substance Use, and Suicidal Ideation During the COVID-19 Pandemic – United States, June 24-30, 2020*, Morbidity and Mortality Weekly

Report, Centers for Disease Control and Prevention, August 2020. Retrieved from: https://www.cdc.gov/mmwr/volumes/69/wr/mm6932a1.htm

64 Pieh, C., Budimir, S., Delgadillo, J., Barkham, M., Fontaine, J. and Probst, T. *Mental health during COVID-19 lockdown in the United Kingdom,* Psychosomatic Medicine, October 2020. Retrieved from: https://journals.lww.com/psychosomaticmedicine/Abstract/9000/Mental_health_during_COVID_19_lockdown_in_the.98497.aspx

65 *Coronavirus: Mental Health in the Pandemic,* Mental Health Foundation UK. Retrieved from: https://www.mentalhealth.org.uk/our-work/research/coronavirus-mental-health-pandemic

66 Price, S. *Touch starvation is a consequence of COVID-19's physical distancing,* Texas Medical Center, May 2020. Retrieved from: https://www.tmc.edu/news/2020/05/touch-starvation

67 Ibid

68 Ducharme, J. *How to Soothe Your 'Re-Entry Anxiety' as COVID-19 Lockdowns Lift,* Time, June 2020. Retrieved from: https://time.com/5850143/covid-19-re-entry-anxiety

69 Ibid

70 *Mental Health at Work During COVID-19,* Paychex, July 2020. Retrieved from: https://www.paychex.com/articles/human-resources/mental-health-at-work-during-covid19

71 *The Imposter Syndrome Epidemic,* The Hub Events, November 2019. Retrieved from: https://www.thehubevents.com/resources/imposter-syndrome-infographic-125

72 Friedman, R.A. *What social isolation may be doing to our brains,* The Washington Post, June 2020. Retrieved from: https://www.washingtonpost.com/opinions/2020/06/12/what-social-isolation-may-be-doing-our-brains

73 *What is survivor's guilt?* Medical News Today, June 2019. Retrieved from: https://www.medicalnewstoday.com/articles/325578#summary

74 Juan, K. *Working While Black: Stories from black corporate America,* Fortune Magazine, June 2020. Retrieved from: https://fortune.com/longform/working-while-black-in-corporate-america-racism-microaggressions-stories

75 Madison, B. September 2020. Retrieved from: https://www.
linkedin.com/posts/bluehairedrecruiter_blacklivesmatter-
blackgirlmagic-blackexcellence-activity-6705855026482491393-
5ul8

76 Linton, Dr. B. *How Companies Can Support Black Employees'
Mental Health in 2020 and Beyond*, Lyra Health, July 2020.
Retrieved from: https://www.lyrahealth.com/blog/how-to-
support-black-employees-mental-health

77 Smith-Spark, L. Elbagir N. and Arvanitidis, B. *How Britain failed
to deal with systemic racism*, CNN, June 2020. Retrieved from:
https://www.cnn.com/2020/06/22/europe/black-britain-systemic-
racism-cnn-poll-gbr-intl/index.html

78 Ibid endnote 74

79 *'Minority Stress' Is Causing More Men to Live Shorter Lives*,
Healthline. Retrieved from: https://www.healthline.com/health-
news/minority-stress#6

80 Jay, L. *Why race matters when it comes to mental health*, BBC,
August 2020. Retrieved from: https://www.bbc.com/future/
article/20200804-black-lives-matter-protests-race-mental-health-
therapy

81 Holman, Dr. A. *Self-Care for Black Americans Amid Race-Based
Traumatic Stress*, Lyra Health, June 2020. Retrieved from: https://
www.lyrahealth.com/blog/self-care-for-black-americans-amid-
race-based-traumatic-stress

82 Neal-Barnett, Dr. A. *How Organizations Can Support the Mental
Health of Black Employees*, Harvard Business Review, June 2020.
Retrieved from: https://hbr.org/
2020/06/how-organizations-can-support-the-mental-health-of-
black-employees

83 Ibid

84 Ibid

85 Ibid

86 Kelly, S. *Woulda, coulda, shoulda: the haunting regret of failing
our ideal selves*, Cornell University, May 2018. Retrieved from:
https://news.cornell.edu/stories/2018/05/woulda-coulda-
shoulda-haunting-regret-failing-our-ideal-selves

USEFUL RESOURCES

GENERAL MENTAL HEALTH AND MENTAL ILLNESS EDUCATION

Global
- World Health Organization: www.who.int/health-topics/mental-health
- United Nations: www.un.org/development/desa/disabilities/issues/mental-health-and-development.html

United States
- Mental Health America: www.mhanational.org
- US Department of Health & Human Services: www.mentalhealth.gov
- National Alliance on Mental Illness (NAMI): www.nami.org
- National Institute of Mental Health: www.nimh.nih.gov
- Centers for Disease Control & Prevention: www.cdc.gov/mentalhealth/index.htm

North and South America
- Pan American Mental Health Organization: www.paho.org

UK and Europe
- Mind UK: www.mind.org.uk
- Mental Health Foundation UK: ww.mentalhealth.org.uk
- Public Health England: publichealthmatters.blog.gov.uk
- Mental Health Europe: www.mhe-sme.org

Australia and New Zealand

o Mental Health Australia: mhaustralia.org
o Australia Government Department of Health: www.health.gov.au/health-topics/mental-health
o Government of Western Australia: www.cci.health. wa.gov.au/Resources/Looking-After-Yourself
o Mental Health Foundation of New Zealand: www.mentalhealth.org.nz
o Community & Public Health New Zealand: www.cph.co.nz/your-health/mental-illness
o New Zealand Ministry of Health: www.health.govt.nz/ your-health/services-and-support/health-care-services/ mental-health-services

RACISM, MENTAL HEALTH AND BEING AN ALLY

o Mental Health America: www.mhanational.org/racism-and-mental-health
o US National Library of Medicine at the National Institutes of Health: www.ncbi.nlm.nih.gov/pmc/ articles/PMC6532404
o Medical News Today: www.medicalnewstoday.com/ articles/racism-and-mental-health#short-term-effects
o The Muse: www.themuse.com/advice/anti-racist-actions-at-work
o Harvard Business Review: www.hbr.org/2020/07/how-to-be-a-better-ally-to-your-black-colleagues

IMPOSTER SYNDROME

o National Public Radio (NPR): www.npr.org/2021/01/22/959656202/5-steps-to-shake-the-feeling-that-youre-an-impostor
o Psychology Today: www.psychologytoday.com/us/ basics/imposter-syndrome

o The Muse: www.themuse.com/advice/the-3-best-moves-to-make-when-youre-dealing-with-imposter-syndrome

o Thrive Global: www.thriveglobal.com/stories/3-ways-to-overcome-imposter-syndrome-while-working-remotely

o Marie Claire UK: www.marieclaire.co.uk/life/work/how-to-combat-imposter-syndrome-when-wfh-706324

TriggerHub.org is one of the most elite and scientifically proven forms of mental health intervention

Trigger Publishing is the leading independent mental health and wellbeing publisher in the UK and US. Clinical and scientific research conducted by assistant professor Dr Kristin Kosyluk and her highly acclaimed team in the Department of Mental Health Law & Policy at the University of South Florida (USF), as well as complementary research by her peers across the US, has independently verified the power of lived experience as a core component in achieving mental health prosperity. Specifically, the lived experiences contained within our bibliotherapeutic books are intrinsic elements in reducing stigma, making those with poor mental health feel less alone, providing the privacy they need to heal, ensuring they know the essential steps to kick-start their own journeys to recovery, and providing hope and inspiration when they need it most.

Delivered through TriggerHub, our unique online portal and accompanying smartphone app, we make our library of bibliotherapeutic titles and other vital resources accessible to individuals and organizations anywhere, at any time and with complete privacy, a crucial element of recovery. As such, TriggerHub is the primary recommendation across the UK and US for the delivery of lived experiences.

At Trigger Publishing and TriggerHub, we proudly lead the way in making the unseen become seen. We are dedicated to humanizing mental health, breaking stigma and challenging outdated societal values to create real action and impact. Find out more about our world-leading work with lived experience and bibliotherapy via triggerhub. org, or by joining us on:

🐦 @triggerhub_

f @triggerhub.org

📷 @triggerhub_

Printed in the USA
CPSIA information can be obtained
at www.ICGtesting.com
JSHW011738120224
57193JS00011B/72